Coun
~ in ~
NEW YORK CITY

A Guide Book
from Country Roads Press

Country Days
~ in ~
NEW YORK CITY

Divya Symmers

Illustrated by
Victoria Sheridan

Country Roads Press
CASTINE · MAINE

Country Days in New York City
© 1993 by Divya Symmers. All rights reserved.

Published by Country Roads Press
P.O. Box 286, Lower Main Street
Castine, Maine 04421

Text and cover design by Edith Allard.
Illustrations by Victoria Sheridan

Reproduction of the 1863 Currier & Ives lithograph, "The Skating Pool, Central Park, Winter," courtesy of The New-York Historical Society, New York, N.Y.

Library of Congress Catalog No.

ISBN 1-56626-030-2

Printed in the United States of America.
10 9 8 7 6 5 4 3 2 1

Library of Congress Cataloging-in-Publication Data

Symmers, Divya.
    Country days in New York City / by Divya Symmers.
        p.   cm.
    Includes bibliographical references and index.
    ISBN 1-56626-030-2 : $9.95
    1. New York (N.Y.)—Guidebooks.   2. Outdoor life—
New York (N.Y.)—Guidebooks.   I. Title.
    F128.18.S96   1993
    917.47′10443—dc20   93-29547
                                                          CIP

For my parents

Contents

Introduction

"There is no greenery. It is enough to make a stone sad."
That's what Nikita Khrushchev said when he came to New York in 1960. He was misinformed. Although the city may be better known for stock markets, sidewalks, and hard-nosed financial deals, it's also a place of colonial farmhouses, Indian caves, and hiking trails; you can find 26,000 acres of parklands,15 miles of beaches, and almost 3 million trees, including the 700,000 or so that line the 6,400 miles of streets.

Statistics aside, you can listen to bluegrass music in Brooklyn, explore a forest or two in Manhattan, take a hayride in Queens, catch a fishing boat in the Bronx, and go back in time at a seventeenth-century village on Staten Island. Square dances, harvest fairs, and homegrown produce may be a relatively hidden element of contemporary life here, but they're as much a part of it as Broadway shows and four-star French restaurants.

Not far from the bustle and brio of midtown Manhattan, communities like Broad Channel and City Island offer a refreshingly small-town ambience. Only a subway and/or bus ride away there are historic nineteenth-century mansions, manicured formal gardens as beautiful as any in the world, and wildlife preserves whose landscapes haven't changed since the first explorers came sailing into New York Harbor.

Back in 1626, when Peter Minuit traded twenty-four dollars' worth of beads and trinkets to local Indians—for what they thought was temporary use of the island—this was a land of forests, ponds, and dramatic rocky hills. A seaside village in the late 1700s (confined to ten blocks between the Battery and Wall Street), by the 1850s the town sprawled beyond 14th Street; in another fourteen years, more than half the population lived above this former boundary. Railroads helped make farther inroads, and as the city spread north farms were swallowed up by brownstones and tenements, lakes and swamps were filled in, and freshwater brooks were smothered by layers of concrete and asphalt.

But somewhere beneath the pavement there still beats a country heart; if you listen on a quiet summer night you might hear it, not quite hidden under the hum of traffic, in the call of a lonely gull soaring over Battery Park, the sound of waves lapping against a dilapidated pier in Brooklyn, or the wild screech of a falcon soaring to its nest in a high-rise on the Upper East Side.

New York City's country roads—historic, off the beaten track, often metaphorical, always intriguing—are waiting to be explored.

The New York City Convention and Visitors Bureau (Two Columbus Circle, New York, NY 10019; telephone 212-397-8222) has maps, brochures, and information on city-wide festivals, special events, hotels, restaurants, transportation—and more.

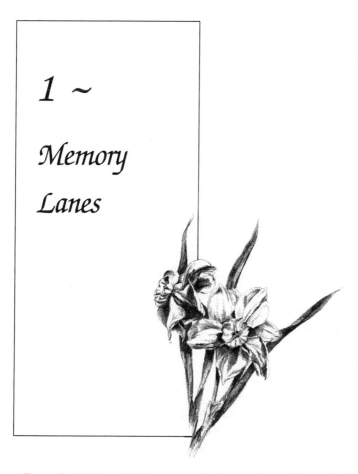

1 ~

Memory Lanes

All roads in New York were country roads, at least in the beginning. In 1609, when Henry Hudson sailed up the mouth of the river that bears his name, the island of Manhattan was a rich hunting and fishing ground for several Algonquin tribes. Trails ran the length of the island, which was covered with thick canopies of forest and crisscrossed by freshwater streams. It was, he wrote, "as beautiful a land as one can hope to tread on."

Although Hudson's ship, the *Half Moon*, moored at the northern tip of the island, the early Dutch settlers chose the southern end to settle on, first establishing a camp on

Governors Island, later erecting Fort Amsterdam at a point overlooking the harbor. There, sometime in the summer of 1626, Peter Minuit—the newly appointed director general of New Netherland—made what might be considered the deal of that or any other century. As a letter sent to officials at the Hague put it: "Our people there are of good cheer and live peaceably. They have bought the island Manhattes . . . for the value of sixty guilders."

One of the best views of the way it used to be is the slightly dusty diorama of New York in the 1660s that's tucked in a forgotten corner of the Museum of Natural History. The walls of Fort Amsterdam are barely visible; the tiny patch of Bowling Green, where Dutch sportsmen gathered for lawn bowling, is in the foreground; and Broadway is just a narrow dirt lane that stretches past a row of small houses. You can almost smell the woodsmoke.

Broadway was more than New Amsterdam's main street in those days. It followed the route of a Native American trail that ran across tree-swathed hills from the Battery to Canal Street, stretching for seventeen miles from the southern tip of the island to its northern boundaries. Today it weaves through Fort Tryon Park along the route of the old Kingsbridge Road, which itself followed a path used by the Weckquaesgeek Indians and connected with a network of trails that led as far north as Albany (and as the Albany Post Road formed what one historian has called a "175-mile street").

Even now, no place evokes the city's past better than the corner of lower Manhattan where Broadway gets its start. Near the Bowling Green subway station, a flagpole is inscribed (in Dutch on one side and English on the other): "On the 22nd of April 1625 the Amsterdam Chamber of Commerce of the West India Company decreed the establishment of Fort Amsterdam and the creation of adjoining farms. . . ."

The fence that surrounds Bowling Green itself is one of the city's oldest standing structures, though the crowns that once capped its iron spikes were removed by patriots in 1776—and, according to legend, melted down for bullets. Except for a couple of homeless men, however, the city's first public park seems to be mostly ignored by the weekday crowds of office workers. Shoo away the pigeons roosting on a nearby plaque and you'll find it was created "for the beauty and ornament of the said street, as well as for the recreation and delight of the inhabitants." Directly opposite—on the site of the original Fort Amsterdam, where Minuit is said to have purchased Manhattan—the old U.S. Customs House is the appropriate new home of the George Gustav Heye Center of the Smithsonian's National Museum of the American Indian. Designed by Cass Gilbert and built in 1907, the imposing beaux-arts structure's interior rotunda is etched with the names of early European explorers, men whose adventuresome spirits led (however inadvertently) to the demise of the island's original culture. At least 900 items from the museum's permanent collection of more than a million artifacts are due to be displayed here; the rest will be eventually relocated to facilities in Washington, D.C., and Maryland from the old Museum of the American Indian on the Upper West Side, and from the museum's research center in the Bronx. Call 212-283-2420 for more information.

Almost as old as Broadway, Pearl Street was originally paved with mother of pearl and oyster shells. Broad Street, then called Heere Graft, edged a canal that ran from the harbor up to what's now Exchange Place. And the corner of Pearl and State streets marked the southern boundaries of the city in those days, before landfill extended it through today's Battery Park.

Keep an eye out for New York Unearthed, at 17 State Street. Located on the block before the chapel dedicated to the memory of Elizabeth Ann Seton (the first American-born saint), the sign, though large, is easy to miss. The ground floor of a skyscraper, after all, may seem an unlikely spot for a branch of the South Street Seaport Museum ("the most common reaction is, 'wow, we didn't know this was here,' " admits the museum educator). But step inside and you'll find displays of local archaeological finds, from trading beads to broken Dresden cups; a glass-enclosed conservation laboratory; and a simulated subterranean elevator that descends deep beneath city streets to a computer-generated archaeological dig—complete with sound, motion, and remarkable visual effects. For more information, call 212-363-9372.

Walk north on Pearl Street to Fraunces Tavern, one of the city's best-known survivors of colonial times. In a block of modest red brick buildings surrounded by steel towers, the restaurant is actually on the ground floor of a 1907 reconstruction of the mansion built in 1719 for Stephen De Lancey. In 1862, it was purchased by Samuel Fraunces, a West Indian entrepreneur who turned it into the Queen's Head Tavern and who later served as George Washington's chief steward. On the second floor, the Fraunces Tavern Museum hosts a regular series of special exhibits, as well as two "period rooms" whose treasures include a piece of George Washington's coffin and where, in sprightlier days, the first president gave a farewell address to his troops. Call 212-425-1778 for hours and to find out about current exhibits.

New Amsterdam's first city hall, or Staadt Huys, stood on Pearl Street between Broad Street and Coenties Slip, a man-made harbor whose surrounding warehouses became a refuge for an enclave of artists in the early 1950s. The thirty-story office building at 85 Broad Street, across from Fraunces Tavern, was built over the site of Governor Lovelaces's Tavern, its British successor. A transparent cover set into the sidewalk reveals a few crumbled walls; a nearby plaque explains that "the tavern was built in 1670 . . . remained in use until 1706 . . . and served as a temporary city hall for a short time after 1697, when the first city hall . . . was declared unsafe." The clay tobacco pipes and wine bottles found here, it goes on to say, are proof that the tavern "was a center for business, political and social activities."

The only empty wine bottles you're likely to stumble across at the present-day City Hall (up at the junction of Broadway and Park Row) might be rolling under benches in surrounding City Hall Park. A public space since New York's earliest days, it was used as a pasture by the Dutch, and as a commons and sometimes execution ground by the British. It's also where Alexander Hamilton led a protest against the Boston port tax in 1774, and on July 9, 1776, Washington and his troops first heard the stirring words of the Declaration of Independence.

To get there from Fraunces Tavern, you could turn left at the corner of 85 Broad Street and take a detour up dark, forgotten Stone Street—said to be the city's first paved road— to Hanover Square. A thriving residential and commercial center in those days, the square's main fame now rests with India House, a private maritime club whose purpose is "the encouragement of foreign commerce." Past the statue of Abraham de Peyster, mayor of New York from 1691 to 1697, stay on Pearl Street until you get to the Barclay's Bank building at 75 Wall Street, where two corner windows display some of the 250,000 artifacts uncovered during its construction in 1984. Among them is a fragment of seventeenth-century delftware tile and a tea set that belonged to an eighteenth-century silversmith.

Wall Street, of course, has long been New York's power street, its narrow corridors lined by such financial giants as the Bank of New York (which Alexander Hamilton founded in 1784) and the Citibank Building (which has served as the Merchant's Exchange, the U.S. Customs House, and as headquarters for the former First National City Bank since it was constructed between 1836 and 1842). Even with eyes closed it's hard to imagine that—around 1653 or so—this was the city's northernmost boundary; first a brushwood fence (to keep the cows in), then a wooden palisade (to keep the British out), beyond which stretched an endless vista of meadows, pastures, ponds, and lush green hills.

Following the old fortification's route, Wall Street comes to a halt at Trinity Church, which has stood here in various incarnations since 1697. The adjacent graveyard, a cool, shady oasis, was originally a Dutch burial ground, and includes Alexander Hamilton among its permanent residents. Concerts and recitals are held in the church on a regular basis—and are definitely worth checking out. Just beforehand, at the corner of Wall and Pine streets, Federal Hall National Memorial stands on the site of the first Federal Hall, where George Washington was sworn in as president of the United States on April 30, 1789. Its thirty-one-foot-high Doric columns were said to have been inspired by the Parthenon, and exhibits inside include the plain brown suit the "land-poor" George (who borrowed money to make the trip from Virginia) wore to his inauguration. For more information call 212-264-8711.

When he wasn't conducting the affairs of the nation, dining at the Queens Head Tavern, or entertaining friends at his home on Cherry Street (now the approach to the Brooklyn Bridge), the first president could be found worshiping at his personal pew in St. Paul's Chapel, about five blocks north on Broadway. New York's oldest public building in continuous use, St. Paul's has stood at the corner of Fulton Street since 1766. While the portico and spire were added on sometime between 1784 and 1796, it's otherwise pretty much unchanged: gray stone with red columns on the outside, pale green vaulted ceiling, pastel pink walls, and chandeliers on the inside. Various historic memorabilia are on display in the glass cases set against the back wall.

On July 1, 1898, crowds of revelers thronged City Hall Park, in celebration of the merging of Manhattan, Brooklyn, Staten Island, Queens, and "a portion of Westchester Country" (which later became the Bronx) to form Greater New York. The elegant, Federal-style City Hall, New York City's official seat of government since 1812, was constructed almost at the city's border—which helps explain the fancy marble

Central Park Skaters, 1863. (Courtesy of The New-York Historical Society, New York, N.Y.)

front and less than impressive "freestone" rear that builders figured no one would see.

By 1898, New York had long since spread beyond its original boundaries. What was wilderness when the Dutch settlers arrived had been filled in, cultivated, and paved over, boosted by the addition of railroads and the gradual implementation of the 1811 "grid" plan that imposed a rigid pattern of city streets on curving country lanes, meadows, and farms. But the remote riverside village of Greenwich, a once sleepy hamlet to which wary early New Yorkers fled during frequent epidemics, was to a large extent bypassed as the city marched northward—leaving pockets of tranquillity that give contemporary Greenwich Village its often surprisingly nineteenth-century character.

From Washington Square, a former potter's field then parade ground that, by the 1850s, had become one of the city's most fashionable addresses, you can wander down two of the city's prettiest lanes: Washington Mews and MacDougal Alley, both lined by converted stables. Even prettier is Patchin Place, a tiny cul-de-sac off West 10th Street whose literary residents have included e.e. cummings, John Reed, and bohemian-journalist Djuna Barnes, who wrote that "the Village does not run past Sixth Avenue. It begins somewhere around Twelfth Street and commits suicide at the Battery." Other cobble-stoned byways of Old New York can be discovered throughout Manhattan: off East 36th Street in Murray Hill, for instance, Sniffen Court's row of brick carriage houses look like they belong in an English village, not midtown. And between 86th and 87th streets on the Upper East Side, Henderson Place is a dead end of tiny, romantic row houses that date to 1882.

Over two centuries earlier—on January 22, 1673—the first mail in North America was dispatched by horseback from

New York City along what became known as the Old Boston Post Road, the King's Highway, or simply "the Great Road." By the mid-eighteenth century, when most of the city's population of 30,000 or so lived south of Canal Street, passengers caught the stage to Boston at a tavern at the edge of town. Traveling at a speed of forty miles a day (in good weather) through open countryside—along the rocky predecessor of what's now Third Avenue—they cut through McGowan's Pass, a British fortification during the Revolutionary War that's still visible in today's Central Park, continuing through the rural village of Haarlem and crossing over Spuyten Duyvil Creek via the King's Bridge, paying a toll of "four pence per mile."

Rerouted across the George Washington Bridge in 1934, the Post Road, aka US 1, still passes through parts of the Bronx on its way from Maine to Florida. Close by is another country road of sorts: the Bronx Heritage Trail. Actually a self-guided tour, the "trail" includes the Valentine-Varian House, a 1758 fieldstone farmhouse that's home to the Museum of Bronx History and the Edgar Allan Poe Cottage, a small white frame house at the corner of East Kingsbridge Road and the Grand Concourse.

"No other house in this city," states a brochure from the 1920s "can boast of having sheltered a poet engaged in the composition of poems of such haunting and melancholy beauty and of such enduring worth." The Boston-born Poe moved here in 1846, hoping that the fresh country air of the tiny village of Fordham—with its "pleasant country lanes and paths in all directions"—would restore the health of his young wife and cousin, Virginia Clemm. Although she died in 1847, followed two years later by her husband, by all accounts their life here was a happy one. "So neat, so poor, so unfurnished, and yet so charming a dwelling I never saw," wrote one visitor. The house became a museum in 1917; in the parlor, there's a reproduction of the desk where Poe wrote

"The Bells" and "Annabel Lee." To find out more about the tour, call the Bronx Historical Society at 718-881-8900.

You can travel down another metaphorical country road in Queens, along the Flushing Freedom Mile, actually closer to two miles. The self-guided route takes in the 1661 Bowne House (site of an early Underground Railway way station); and the country's oldest (1694) Quaker meeting house. It also stops at the venerable Weeping Beech tree, a living landmark planted in 1847 that flourishes in a tiny park behind the Kingsland Homestead, built by a Quaker farmer who was one of the first New Yorkers to free his slaves. For more information, call the Queens Historical Society at 718-939-0647.

Several New York roads manage to incorporate parklike elements while actually functioning as routes between one place and another. Parkways, for instance, were the inspiration of Frederick Law Olmsted, who envisioned streets planted with trees and shrubbery connecting all the city's parks (and succeeded in creating Brooklyn's Eastern and Ocean parkways). Robert Moses, the commissioner of parks from 1934 until 1960, not only rammed expressways through parts of New York, he also built a few of its most scenic roads. Among them is the Henry Hudson Parkway which follows the Hudson River's route past the hills and trees of Inwood Hill and Fort Tryon parks, before reaching the George Washington Bridge and sudden city lights.

Other country roads have yet to be paved. The Brooklyn/Queens Greenway, a forty-mile bicycle path described as the urban version of the Appalachian Trail, is scheduled for completion by 1995. On Staten Island, an abandoned railroad line has been optimistically earmarked as a "link in a future greenway between lower Manhattan and New Jersey" as well as a pedestrian-cum-biking trail. And the Bronx Greenway, an idealized eighty miles of walking and biking corridors along waterfront, abandoned railways, streets, and parks, may eventually link the borough with Westchester, Manhattan, and Queens. "Nine of the eleven routes aren't there yet," admits a spokesperson for the project. "There's nothing much to see unless you have a lot of imagination."

Someday, too—according to the Neighborhood Open Space Coalition, an organization dedicated to expanding the city's parks and other open spaces—an emerald necklace may link Manhattan's waterside parks with miles of tree-lined walkways. Already the new Hudson River Park, which the *New York Times* called "a starter emerald," stretches along West Street from Laight to Vesey. From here, you can walk south to Battery Park along the riverside esplanade that starts at the foot of the World Financial Center. Tall lamps cast old-fashioned shadows along the way; cul-de-sacs end in whimsical sculpture gardens—a chess table, a giant living room with granite chairs. Eventually you come to a series of scenic lookouts set amidst artfully landscaped gardens that offer some of the city's most spectacular views of the Statue of Liberty. Here, water, sky, grass, and national monument meet in perfect harmony. "One never need leave the confines of New York," wrote poet Frank O'Hara, in words immortalized in brass on the fence at the esplanade's start, "to get all the greenery one wishes."

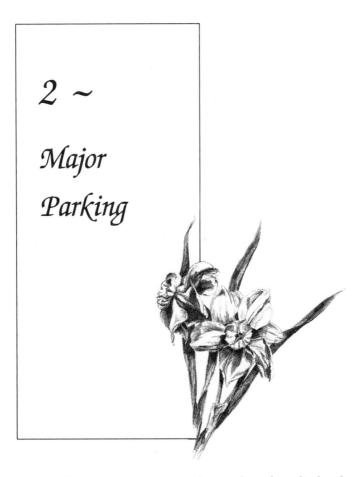

2 ~
Major
Parking

One early autumn morning when only a few die-hard sun worshipers lay on Orchard Beach, I followed a man carrying a couple of fishing poles along the Kazimiroff Nature Trail in Pelham Bay Park. "Mainly bluefish," he said, when asked what he was fishing for. "The only trouble is I'm too early. No water," he gestured to the low-tide mudflats where gulls waddled in search of mussels and other delicacies. A monarch butterfly flickered across the path and settled on the pink and yellow wildflowers clustered at the base of an emergency telephone box. Squirrels rooted in the underbrush; seaweed and smooth sea glass lay in shiny clumps along the shore; and veering inland, the trail passed through a grove of gnarled oaks so thick the sun barely glinted through a bower of green-gold leaves. The air was tanged with salt, and, except for the distant drone of a passing jet, the only sound was the underlying hum of crickets.

Almost 7,000 of New York's more than 26,000 acres of parklands are close to their natural state, and more than 100 of the city's parks are over 20 acres in size. A few are crossed by nature trails that look and feel more like the Catskills or Adirondacks than the country's largest metropolis. Some are on the shore, with beaches as good as you'll find anywhere. Others, like Staten Island's Greenbelt, are shady inland oases that go on for miles. Still others offer tennis, golf, swimming, croquet, and horseback riding, but they all provide something in common: instant relief from the hassles of city life.

Urban Park Rangers

Created in 1979 to provide educational programs and patrol city parks, the Urban Park Rangers lead free nature walks in all five boroughs (see also Chapter 3, "Take a Hike"). Themes range from fall flower tours in Van Cortlandt Park, to winter solstice celebrations in Kissena Park, spring wetlands explorations in Marine Park, and summer hikes through Central Park's North Woods. For a schedule of seasonal walks and workshops in the Bronx, call 718-430-1832; in Brooklyn, 718-287-3400; in Manhattan, 212-427-4040; in Queens, 718-699-4204; in Staten Island, 718-667-6042. At night and on weekends, call 1-800-834-3832.

They say the Bronx got its name when early Manhattanites trekked up to visit a farmer named Jacob Bronck, or Bronk. Whether the story's true or not has been lost in the mists of time and exhaust smoke, but it is a fact that, in those days, the only mainland borough was a verdant land of farms and narrow country lanes. Today, while suffering from a reputation for burned-out buildings and other signs of crumbling urban blight, it's also home to New York's largest expanse of green.

Bordering Westchester County, Pelham Bay Park opened in 1888 and was reached by a succession of public transport, including the New York, New Haven & Hartford Railroad, elevated trains, a monorail, and, starting in 1894, the IRT Subway. Subway is still the easiest way to travel from Manhattan; the IRT No. 6 line's last stop is within walking distance of the visitors' center staffed by Urban Park Rangers. (Call 718-548-7070 for information about current tours, special exhibits, and educational programs.)

No matter how you get there, you may want to stay a while to explore the park's 2,764 acres, which encompass a nineteenth-century mansion, one of the city's most popular public beaches, an environmental center, two golf courses, a couple of wildlife sanctuaries, several nature trails, a stable, bridle paths, and the city's Mounted Police School. The park offers a certain romantic seventeenth-century resonance, too. In 1642, Anne Hutchinson, a religious refugee from the strict Massachusetts Bay Colony for whom the adjacent Hutchinson Parkway and Hutchinson River are named, settled here with a small band of like-minded freethinkers. During attacks by local Indians, understandably hostile at the usurpation of their hunting and fishing grounds, she hid—for a time successfully—in the crevice of a large glacial rock. Although she and most of her followers were later killed, the Split Rock she took refuge in remains a natural monument to an era when this was virgin forest and wetlands. For a glimpse of how it might have been, take the Split Rock trail that travels north past Goose Creek Marsh and through the Thomas Pell Wildlife Sanctuary. You might spot wading herons, sandpipers, and woodcocks.

Beyond Orchard Beach—created from landfill in the 1930s—the Hunter Island Marine Zoology and Geology Sanctuary is a refuge for an amazing variety of bird and animal life, from marsh hawks and graceful snowy egrets to tiny meadow mice. Edged by glacier rocks and boulders believed to be among the oldest on the northeast coast of the United States, it was part of the original land grant given to Thomas Pell, a wealthy English colonist who purchased over 9,000 acres from the Siwanoy Indians in 1654, and eventually declared himself the Lord of Pelham Manor. (The Kazimiroff Nature Trail starts behind the beach.)

Central Park is the best known of the city's green oases. With good reason. Sooner or later almost any movie made here includes a shot of trees and fields backed by that unmistakably urban silhouette of clifflike apartment buildings. It's also one of New York's most underrated natural resources: In winter, rabbits leave paw prints in the snow; in fall and spring, thousands of birds stop off on their way south or north. Raccoons peer from hidden burrows in summer, when concerts on the Great Lawn attract up to a million people. Even the weather's supposed to be a good ten degrees cooler than in the rest of Manhattan. No matter how crowded it gets, there are plenty of hidden nooks where you can rest undisturbed by the masses roller-blading, jogging, and sunbathing around you. This, after all, not only was the country's first park, it was the world's first major park created expressly *for* the masses.

To Frederick Law Olmsted, who designed it with architect Calvert Vaux, the purpose was to "supply hundreds of thousands of tired workers, who have no opportunity to spend summers in the country, a specimen of God's handiwork." Actually, the handiwork was Olmsted and Vaux's, who supervised the dislodgment of thousands of tons of earth and the planting of almost as many trees and shrubs in order to transform what was, until the mid-nineteenth century, a swampy tract of mostly flat no-man's-land into a spectacular,

Cascades in Central Park

843-acre "natural" vista that includes lakes, streams, gardens, meadows, lawns, over a hundred acres of woodlands, fifty-eight miles of winding footpaths and a four-mile-long bridle path that's been called "the prettiest country road in New York City." (Horses can be rented from the Upper West Side's Claremont Riding Academy; call 212-724-5100.)

From the entrance at Fifth Avenue and 59th Street, follow the path past the zoo and the Wollman Rink (ice skating in winter, roller-skating and miniature golf the rest of the year) to the Dairy, a Victorian Gothic structure that was an integral part of the park's original Children's District. In the late nineteenth century, cows and milkmaids were placed here so that city kids could taste fresh milk, often for the first time in their lives. Now it's the Central Park Visitor Center (212-794-6564), where you can pick up copies of a handy pedestrian map and the self-guided walking tour that ultimately leads to Bethesda Terrace and Bethesda Fountain.

The formal terrace and intricately sculpted fountain were a contribution of Calvert Vaux's, and undoubtedly the part that Frederick Olmsted, whose vision it was to keep the park as natural and wild as possible, liked least. However, they're definitely elegant, if crowded on weekends, and overlook the lake, where you can rent a rowboat or hire a gondola and imagine you're in Venice. Cross the Bow Bridge from here and you'll soon arrive at the park's "wild heart." The Ramble is a thirty-seven-acre sylvan interlude of narrow, winding paths, natural streams, overgrown thickets, and a century-old cedar-wood rustic shelter—the last of several that used to perch on rocky outcrops. You'll feel light-years away from the rest of the city. (Because it is so secluded, park officials recommend that you walk with friends here and on other less-traveled paths.)

At the north end of the Ramble, just above the 79th Street transverse, Belvedere Castle rises in gothic majesty atop Vista Rock. Built in 1872, it's home to a learning center that offers ecology courses, a National Weather Service station, and one of the city's better views. Beyond the reservoir shimmering in the distance, you can barely make out the shadow of the North Woods, a remote overgrown forest between 102d and 106th streets that sounds like it belongs in Minnesota, not New York City. Once there you'll find that trails run through a mysteriously deep ravine, alongside a romantic loch, and past a series of small, tumbling waterfalls before meeting at Glen Span at one end and Huddlestone Arch (both rustic stone bridges) at the other. Escorted tours of the North Woods are recommended, either with the Urban Park Rangers or the Parks Administration (212-427-4040 or 212-360-2766). One of the newest modes of transportation in the city is the Conservancy Trolley, which offers an hour-and-a-half in-depth look at Central Park's best- and lesser-known attractions (for details, call 212-360-2727). The oldest way to get around is provided by the famous horse-drawn carriages that wait for passengers along Central Park South.

Across the East River from Manhattan, Queens is "New York City's greenest borough, with over 7,000 acres of parkland and 52 percent of all the street trees," says a former Urban Park Ranger now with the Department of Parks and Recreation. Like many Queens residents, she's miffed that even native New Yorkers aren't aware that at least 10 percent of the city's largest borough is composed of natural attractions like Forest Park's stand of tall oaks and Alley Pond Park's nature trails (see Chapter 3, "Take a Hike").

With close to 1,300 acres of grassy meadows, a lake you can boat on, and a small but pleasant wetlands preserve, Flushing Meadows—Corona Park is not only Queens' most sizable, but the second biggest city park. Former site of the 1939 and 1964 World's Fairs, once upon a time it was a swamp, then a municipal garbage dump. Nowadays it's home to a dazzling array of cultural institutions, including the New York

Hall of Science and the Queens Museum. It's also New York's hometown "sports central," where you can watch tennis greats vie for the title at the U.S. Open and root, however futilely, for the Mets to win the pennant.

As if Shea Stadium weren't enough, the park contains more recreational facilities than the average small country: Miles (and miles) of gently rolling bike paths, a sailing school, a pitch-and-putt golf course, an enormous indoor ice-skating rink, and year-round tennis at the USTA National Tennis Center—except at the end of the summer, when the champs take the courts. For information and directions, call 718-760-6561.

Queens may be the greenest borough, but within Brooklyn's 73 square miles are 400 parks that add up to at least 4,000 acres of parkland. The largest is 798-acre Marine Park, mainly saltwater wetlands with baseball fields and tennis courts (a dozen each), picnic lawns, a couple of bocce courts, a public golf course, and three cricket fields carved from old farmland and turn-of-the-century landfill. Centuries ago, Native Americans fished here. Later, Dutch settlers harvested oysters along the shore. Today, although it's one of the city's officially designated natural areas—and not far from the seafood restaurants and fishing boats of Sheepshead Bay—Marine Park remains relatively unknown to all but neighborhood residents. So does the mile-long Gerritsen Creek Nature Trail, which passes by the submerged remains of a gristmill—the country's first—that ground grain here from about 1645 until 1889. There's a sadly vandalized viewing platform about halfway; if you're lucky you might see herons and egrets in summer, loons and Canada geese during the winter months, and in spring and fall, plovers, sandpipers, and other shorebirds. To find out when the next escorted walk is scheduled, call the Brooklyn Urban Park Rangers at 718-287-3400.

Deer used to graze on the meadows of Prospect Park, by far the borough's most famous outdoor attraction. Years later, a rogue fox was rumored to roam the 526-acre park's rugged woods. Along with Manhattan's Central Park, Prospect Park is the result of the visionary designs of Frederick Law Olmsted and Calvert Vaux; some consider it their crowning achievement. Created between 1866 and 1874 (when Brooklyn was still a city separate from New York), it was intended to blend trees, lakes, and fields in a way that immediately thrust the visitor into a country environment. If the recent Urban Park Ranger program on "Winter Wildlife Survival Techniques" is any indication, the plan succeeded.

There's information about nature walks and other free programs (plus maps that guide you to the popular Kate Wollman skating rink and other attractions) at the Boathouse Visitors Center, overlooking the Lullwater, which branches off sixty-acre Prospect Lake. On weekends, stop at the charming carousel—restored to its original 1912 glory a couple of years ago—and ride a hand-carved giraffe, lion, deer, or one of fifty-four wooden Arabian stallions with real horsehair tails. You can also rent a real steed (call 718-851-9230 to find out how) and take off along the Bridle Path, which winds around the lake, past the fairy-tale-sounding Nethermead. The Urban Park Rangers also lead walks through the Ravine, a woodland gully where the appearance of a troll or two wouldn't be surprising.

From the entrance at Grand Army Plaza, follow the path that leads to the park's Long Meadow, and you'll see what Olmsted meant when he wrote that "the occasional contemplation of natural scenes . . . is favorable to the health and vigor of men." The surrounding streets seem to suddenly evaporate. In their place is an inspiring, expansive field of rolling green that disappears—along with any lingering stress—into a dark ridge of distant trees. For general information, call 718-965-8951; for weekly events, 718-788-0055.

Prospect Park Boat House

Surprisingly, the city has five—mainly recreational—
state parks, including a new one on top of a Harlem sewage-
treatment plant that may be the ultimate example of recycling.
Just over the Verrazano-Narrows Bridge, Staten Island is
home to perhaps the most scenic: a former clay-mining site on

21

the southwest shore that time has transformed into a refuge for muskrats, rabbits, raccoons, black snakes, box turtles, and other wildlife. Accessible by S-74 bus from the ferry terminal, some of Clay Pit Ponds State Park Preserve's 260 acres of fragile wetlands, woods, and sandy barrens are off limits, but most can be explored on trails that stay open from sunrise to sunset. There's a rich program of nature walks, crafts, and storytelling for children, too; call 718-967-1976 for details.

On the way back toward the Verrazano Bridge, the beach and boardwalk of Great Kills Park look out at New York Harbor—and are just one part of the 26,000 acres that belong to the Gateway National Recreation Area. It may come as another surprise, but this is the country's only urban national park: a four-part patchwork of forest, beach, and wetlands that extends along the harbor coastline from Sandy Hook, New Jersey, to Breezy Point, on the Rockaway Peninsula. On a humid weekday afternoon, the prospect of four and a half miles of uninterrupted sand drew me past the more crowded Rockaways, toward historic Fort Tilden, to the (sometimes) more secluded dunes of Gateway's Jacob Riis Park. For what seemed hours, hardly anyone walked by; just sun, sea, and swooping gulls. For information, call the Breezy Point Unit at 718-318-4300 or Gateway's headquarters at 718-338-3338. Or write to: Gateway National Recreation Area Headquarters, Floyd Bennett Field, Brooklyn, NY 11234.

3 ~

Take a Hike

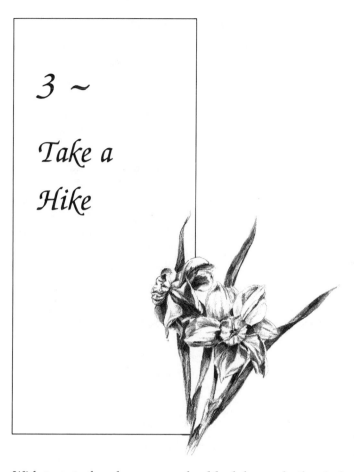

With twenty-four-hour gyms, health clubs, and other indoor centers of exercise in abundance, sometimes we need reminding that the great outdoors offers even more spacious opportunities for stretching legs (and other bodily parts). It seems that everyone in New York jogs: Take a run around Central Park's Reservoir any Sunday morning and it looks like half the city's in training for the next marathon. But you don't have to trek up to the Adirondacks for a walk in the woods. There are plenty of trails right here. Some are short, scenic bridle paths well trod by foot and hoof; others stretch for six or seven wild and overgrown miles; and a couple keep on going (and going) beyond the city limits like an Energizer battery commercial.

The so-called forgotten borough of Staten Island, for instance, is more than the home of the world's largest landfill or notorious Mafia chieftains. It's also where you'll find the Greenbelt: 2,500 acres of parkland that make up the city's largest contiguous open space—and includes four major color-blazed paths that connect and double back to create more than thirty miles of hiking trails. Before 1964, when the Verrazano-Narrows Bridge linked Staten Island with Brooklyn, this was still a relatively underpopulated community with a few real working farms and miles of native forest. Developed to retain (and in some instances, reclaim) that country heritage, today Staten Island's natural "green belt" is happily available to city hikers, cross-country skiers, bird-watchers, and other intrepid explorers.

All roads—or in this case, all trails—meet at or pass through High Rock Park, a 90-acre nature preserve that was a Girl Scout camp until 1964 (New York City's only Boy Scout camp still abuts the property). To get there, take the S-74 bus from the Staten Island Ferry Terminal to the corner of Richmond Road and Rockland Avenue, then either change to an S-54 or walk north on Rockland three blocks to Nevada Avenue. The sign for High Rock is on your left; Nevada is on your right and leads up through a hillside neighborhood of tidy houses with imaginative gardens to the park's wire-fence entrance. The transition is startling: A canopy of trees so thick that even in a sudden summer rainfall you hardly feel a drop. Birds by the hundreds fill the air with trills and squawks; you can barely hear the muffled drone of a buzz saw off in the distance. Even the narrow asphalt road (speed limit: 5 mph) up to the Greenbelt administration office seems enchanted, while the office itself is a low-slung wood-and-stone cabin that looks like something out of Hansel and Gretel.

Greenbelt Headquarters

The Staten Island Urban Park Rangers are based in another nearby cottage and offer a year-round series of weekend programs that range from searching for wild mushrooms to spotting rare songbirds. There's also a small Environmental Education Center where kids learn about the Greenbelt's abundance of plant and animal life. Stop in at the Visitor Center for a trail map and Greenbelt guide. Located in a former chicken coop, it includes an "environmentally responsible" gift shop where you can buy jars of High Rock honey, courtesy of the industrious bees that live in adjacent hives. While you're at it, take a look at the back-room art exhibits; emphasizing natural themes, all works are done by local artists. When I was there, the exhibit included pottery made out of clay from Central Park.

Because a glacier ridge runs right through the middle of Staten Island, the trails pass through New York's highest hills—which means plenty of spectacular vistas. In winter, when the trees are bare, even the windows of the High Rock Administration Center boast a splendid view of Raritan Bay. From here, you can hike part of the 8.5-mile-long Blue Trail, which climbs Todt Hill—the highest point on the Eastern Seaboard between Maine and New Jersey—before continuing along a forested ridge to Clove Lakes Park, where another woodland trail meanders through a forest of towering oaks. En route, there's a scenic overlook from which you can see the highlands of New Jersey. The Yellow Trail connects with the other end of the Blue Trail at Latourette Park, site of one of the city's few public 18-hole golf courses and a popular place for winter sledding and skiing. Or take the White Trail south from Willowbrook, a mainly recreational park with its own fishing pond, to Great Kills Park, where fresh ocean breezes await you. Except for occasional paved-road interruptions, you're surrounded by deep woods as you journey north to south, hooking up with the Blue Trail near Rockland Avenue or continuing into the Egbertville Ravine.

If just getting to Staten Island has worn you out, High Rock's 90 acres also encompass shorter but just as sweet paths, including the Swamp Trail which starts not far from the park's entrance, off the narrow access road. First you'll see a clearing that looks like a meadow but is actually a water-soggy swamp filled with turtles, redwing blackbirds, possums, chipmunks, squirrels, (nonpoisonous) water snakes, and an astounding array of fungi. Then the one-mile trail circumnavigates the swamp and seems to take you into one of Jules Verne's fabled lost worlds; moisture-laden branches brush your face, the ground sinks lightly beneath your feet with each step. Across one of several plank bridges there's a small clearing where a semicircle of large granite rocks sits like something left over from ancient Druidic rites. For more information about the Greenbelt, call 718-667-2165 or the Staten Island Urban Park Rangers at 718-667-6042.

The faint indent of old wagon trails can be found in Alley Pond Park; remnants of the days when a small settlement stood in "the Alley" itself—a narrow slice of creeks, ponds, and wetlands that lies at the junction of Little Neck Bay and Alley Creek. In the 1920s, when the city first acquired this parcel of land in northeastern Queens, a general store still stood here; since then, the Long Island Expressway and two adjoining parkways have chopped the 654-acre park into over a dozen separate parcels of land. For visiting purposes, there are two major divisions, both accessible by a combination of subway and bus, or car. At the top end, off Northern Boulevard, the Alley Pond Environmental Center (718-229-4000) offers ecology courses and trail walks through fresh- and saltwater marshland, where wildlife ranges from mallards to muskrats to black-crowned night herons. You can hike around most of it on the two-mile Pitobik Trail. The bottom end, off Grand Central Parkway (Winchester Boulevard exit), is where a short path between the Alley Athletic Park building and tennis courts leads to the last remaining stretch of the Old Vanderbilt Motor Parkway, constructed by William K. Vanderbilt, Jr., in 1908 so he'd have a place to race his fleet of (then) state-of-the-art motorcars. The now empty asphalt road used to cover forty-eight miles; what's left is a wonderfully overgrown two-mile stretch, edged by black locust trees, tangled underbrush, and wildflowers, that travels under graffiti-painted underpasses to the edge of Cunningham Park, about a forty-five-minute walk.

You might spot a stray Connecticut warbler along the way, but most songbirds hover around the glacial ponds of Alley Pond Park's southern forest, a hundred acres of oak, beech, sweet gum, and flowering dogwood that stretches north of the Grand Central Parkway to the Long Island Expressway. The Urban Park Rangers lead walks here and along the Kissena Corridor, Queens' own strip of "greenbelt" that tenuously connects Alley Pond with the forested trails of Cunningham and Kissena parks, and ultimately with Flushing Meadows. Call 718-699-4204 for information.

Long before the turn of the century, you could keep walking north past 110th Street—where Central Park ends—through meadows, farmland, and a series of sleepy hamlets all the way to Spuyten Duyvil, the narrow channel that joins the Hudson with the Harlem River. On the way, you'd run into a 260-foot-high hill that was the site of a fierce Revolutionary War battle and these days is better known as the site of the Cloisters (see Chapter 5, "Gardens of Urban Delight"). Fort Tryon Park's rocky heights, landscaped gardens, and lofty views also offer seekers of solitude several trails and paths to explore, now handily accessible by the A train to 190th Street.

On the other side of Dyckman Street, Inwood Hill Park stretches north to Spuyten Duyvil, where Henry Hudson landed in 1609, and where Manhattan ends. Like most great ending places, Inwood Hill is a place where history and geology meet, in this case to create the city's most remote, romantic park. Once wolves roamed free and Native Americans held sway in the great forest here, part of which remains as Manhattan's last stand of native oak, hickory, and tulip trees. Later, stagecoaches stopped at the nearby Blue Bell Tavern to rest their horses before continuing the long journey from New York to Boston. "It's one of the most isolated places on the island of Manhattan," says Larry Scoones, former director of special projects for New York's Urban Park Rangers.

The best way to experience Inwood Hill's ancient cliffs and strangely poignant wilderness is by exploring the park's ten-plus miles of trails, preferably with a friend or two. Although no up-to-date maps or guides exist as yet, most trails are clearly marked. From the ravine on the far side of the marsh that curves in from Spuyten Duyvil, next to a playing field, you can climb to the top of Inwood Hill, where the reward is a wide, windswept view across the Hudson to New Jersey's palisades. At the base of the hill—not far from a middens where oyster shells as big as dinner plates have been found—caves used by hunting parties of Weckquaesgeek Indians are scattered amidst rocky outcrops. This part of the park—indeed, all of Inwood Hill's 100 acres of woodlands—was recently renamed the Shorakapok Natural Area, in honor of the Indian village that, long ago, stood between what's now 204th and 207th streets. An annual Native American festival (see Chapter 10, "Fairs and Festivals") also takes place here and by 1994, an urban ecology center will hopefully be set up in an old boathouse by the freshwater marsh, near the 218th Street entrance. For more information, contact the Inwood Heights Parks Alliance (212-304-0730), a neighborhood group that offers environmental programs and walks. The Urban Park Rangers also lead guided walks here and in neighboring Fort Tryon Park; call 212-427-4040.

If you continued north from the Bronx side of the Harlem River, you'd reach the southern tip of Riverdale Park at West 232d Street and Palisade Avenue. The narrow strip of cotton-woods, maples, and mulberries that stretches—with one interruption—along the river to 254th Street is another of the city's most secluded secrets: woods and wetland trails, created from privately owned land between 1942 and 1952.

Bird-watchers come here to admire double-crested cormorants and migrating hawks; naturalists are drawn by a myriad of native and nonnative plants; and archaeologists have discovered a number of ancient and colonial-era sites. The park's northern oaks border the grounds of Wave Hill (see Chapter 8, "A House in the Country"), not far from Metro-North's Riverdale Station. The Urban Park Ranger's Van Cortlandt Park office has a current schedule of walks; call 718-548-7070.

A short distance away, Van Cortlandt Park is New York's third largest green space. Possibly the one with the most historic sites, too: The list includes a mansion where George Washington slept, the ancient site of an Indian village, the largest freshwater lake in the Bronx plus two golf courses and a riding stable, all within almost 1,200 acres that border Broadway from West 240th to West 263d streets. Despite the fact that it's traversed by the Major Deegan Expressway and both the Mosholu and Henry Hudson parkways, it also has some of the city's longest, most noteworthy hiking trails.

The Old Putnam Railroad Track, a defunct railroad bed that one Manhattan-based Urban Park Ranger tells me is his favorite walk in the city ("I love being out in the fresh New York air," he adds), follows the route of a commuter train that ran from the Bronx up to Brewster, New York, for almost a century. Now that the "Old Put," as commuters called it, is no longer in use, rabbits, skunks, and raccoons have taken over. Even deer and foxes have been spotted, and the variety of birdlife waiting to be spotted along the way includes the occasional rare great horned owl.

On the shorter side, the John Kieran Nature Trail meanders along one side of Van Cortlandt Lake, through a patch of freshwater marshland—about a forty-five minute walk. The Cass Gallagher Nature Trail is another relatively short stroll that passes through a 200-year-old hardwood forest inhabited by skunks, pheasants, and raccoons. The big news for hikers, however, is the Croton Aqueduct Trail, which follows the route of the city's first aqueduct system for twenty-five miles, plowing through parts of Yonkers and Westchester County before ending at the Croton Dam. Built in the mid-nineteenth century, after fire and pestilence alerted public officials to the need for a continuous supply of fresh, uncontaminated water, the newly completed course was edged, in those days, by a pleasant footpath much favored by Edgar Allan Poe during his short stay at the little Bronx cottage that now bears his name. You might be inspired, as well. Call the Urban Park Rangers.

If twenty-five miles doesn't sound far enough, consider the Long Path, a 240-mile hike that starts on the New Jersey side of the George Washington Bridge, crosses back into New York state after twelve miles, and ends at the northern end of Catskill Park. Created in the 1930s as a link between various scenic backcountry points of interest, it's now part of 1100 miles of foot trails maintained by the New York–New Jersey Trail Conference, a federation of hiking and outdoors clubs. Members include the New York City chapter of the Appalachian Mountain Club plus the more eclectic-sounding Murray Hill Canoe Club, Country Dance New York, and the Pinewoods Folk Music Club (who bring their instruments with them when they go). The Trail Conference issues a newsletter that lists current walks offered by these and other city hiking groups; recent choices have ranged from a leisurely trek around Brooklyn's oceanside community of Sheepshead Bay to a more ambitious six-mile hike from Riverdale Park to Van Cortlandt Park. To join, call 212-685-9699 or write to: NY-NJ Trail Conference, Room 401, 232 Madison Avenue, New York, NY 10016.

4 ~

Walks on the Wild Side

A city of nightclubs that never close and night crawlers who habitually stay out past dawn, the Big Apple has always been home to wild creatures. The gryphons, dragons, and other mythological beasts that grace the stone façades of some of Manhattan's skyscrapers may be silent, but a few years back the windswept dome of the Cityspire building on West 56th Street developed a life of its own, emitting a whistling sound so loud that city officials were forced to issue an "unnecessary noise" citation. Even Patience and Fortitude, the matching set of stone lions who've guarded the main entrance to the Public Library on 42nd Street since 1911, actually roared at one point, when a realistic tape recording was installed in an attempt to keep them from being vandalized.

Urban folklore abounds with these and other tales, from the ever popular mutant alligators in the sewers to the adventurous colony of ants that supposedly made its home at the highest reaches of the Empire State Building. And while sheep no longer graze on Central Park's Sheep Meadow, the local Audubon Society reports that, in 1992, nine pairs of peregrine falcons tried to set up housekeeping on the uppermost reaches of city "canyons"; seven were successful—including one feathered couple that nested in the lofty recesses of the MetLife Building on Park Avenue. (When the company's logo was installed to replace the old Pan Am sign, consultants were brought in to make sure the graceful raptors weren't unduly disturbed.) Other seasonal wildlife includes the spring parade of pachyderms that stalks majestically through the Queens-Midtown Tunnel and winds slowly but surely to Madison Square Garden—an urban rite of passage that heralds the arrival of the Ringling Brothers Barnum and Bailey Circus. Another comes at the end of every summer, when a smaller bestial procession—from tiny household hamsters to Saint Bernards and a stray camel or two—pads up the center aisle of the Cathedral of St. John the Divine for the annual Blessing of the Animals.

In 1993, the city's zoos were officially retagged "wildlife conservation parks" (partly in an effort to make sure no one confused them with the everyday variety). Whatever they're called, with one for each borough, New York is definitely leader of the pack. In Manhattan, the old Central Park Zoo was a dreary prison for animals that left visitors depressed. Lions sulked behind iron bars in bare cement cages, leopards appeared to be vaguely psychotic, even the monkeys looked annoyed. Totally revamped in the late 1980s, the new and improved Central Park Zoo/Wildlife Center—in the same

33

locale at 64th Street and Fifth Avenue—has become one of Manhattan's most popular minigetaways, a "landscape immersion" experience in which over 450 creatures from more than 130 species enjoy luxurious new habitats spread out over five and a half acres.

Inside the two-level, skylit Tropic Zone's steamy rainforest environment, you'll feel like you're on a quick vacation

Sea lions in their special pool, Central Park

(particularly welcome on frigid, blustery days) in a warmer part of the world. A twenty-foot waterfall cascades into a riverbank stream, and glass-walled exhibits planted with moss and natural greenery reveal everything from sinuous pythons to black-and-white colobus monkeys. "Who does your hair?" mused a hip-looking visitor, lost in admiration at one with a particularly startling thatch of white fur. In the outdoor Temperate Territory, landscaped paths wind past a lake with a mountainous island of Japanese snow monkeys and a smaller pond that's home to frolicking river otters. On humid summer days, the climate-controlled Edge of the Ice-pack exhibit, where penguins and puffins hang out, is one of the best places in town to cool off. So is the adjacent Polar Circle, where you can watch polar bears do the backstroke, from underneath or at eye level, courtesy of multilevel viewing windows. For feeding times at the zoo and other information, call 212-861-6030.

King Kong didn't actually clutch the top of the Empire State Building (though you can pose with his likeness on the eighty-sixth floor), but the lowland gorillas at the Bronx Zoo's Great Ape House look just as, if not more, imposing. Also known as the Bronx Zoo/Wildlife Conservation Park, this is New York's "big zoo," as well as one of the country's oldest. Possibly the only one in the world with a cocktail named after it, too. The story goes that in 1899, right after the zoo opened, a bartender at the Waldorf mixed up a potent concoction of gin, vermouth, and fresh orange juice. The drink proved so popular he named it the Bronx Cocktail because, he said, after just one or two, customers often reported seeing new and unusual creatures.

Rare beasts are par for the course inside this 265-acre wild kingdom, which has over 4,000 of them—some of which you'd have to go 30,000 or more miles to find anywhere else, instead of a relatively quick trip by bus, train, subway, or car.

Snow leopards, close to extinction in the wild, have been exhibited here since 1903, and since 1987 have had their own ersatz Himalayan Highlands habitat complete with tall trees, ravines, and heated rocks for wintertime basking. At the Baboon Reserve, part of the twenty-two-acre Africa exhibit, an old riverbed winds through a grassy hillside harboring a troop of fierce-looking 100-pound Ethiopian gelada baboons. One of the zoo's most popular exhibits is Wild Asia, a forty-acre complex that includes camel rides and the "Bengali Express" monorail that travels for two miles through a natural riverside setting where Siberian tigers, Asian elephants, red pandas, and Indian rhinoceros roam free.

The zoo's Rainey Gate entrance is across Fordham Road from the New York Botanical Garden and leads past an eighteenth-century Italian fountain to the Astor Court garden, where sea lions cavort in a freshwater pool. The palatial beaux arts–style building at the tip of Astor Court, an elephant house since 1908, reopened in 1990 as the Keith W. Johnson Zoo Center. Pick up a self-guided tour map from the glass-walled information area (ask about special events like the occasional early morning elephant baths), then go explore the Zoo Center's luxurious expanded natural habitats for Indian rhinos, Malay tapirs, and Asian elephants. The elephants even have their own woodland pool; you can watch them enjoy it from overlooks set along the path that meanders through a forest of bamboo and rhododendron.

There's much more, of course, including one of the best children's zoos in the country. Plan on spending the whole day if you want to see everything. Call 718-367-1010 for travel directions.

Wild deer have been spotted on Staten Island. So have raccoons, rabbits, and feral cats. An observant trek through the 2,500-acre Greenbelt may reveal these and other animals (see Chapter 3, "Take a Hike"). For a closer look at Staten

Island's muskrats, chipmunks, and thousands of migrating birds (including great blue herons, marsh hawks, egrets, and cranes), try the Greenbelt's William T. Davis Wildlife Refuge, a 260-acre marshland enclave named for the prominent nineteenth-century naturalist who, among other accomplishments, founded the Staten Island Institute of Arts and Sciences in 1881. Bordered by houses on one side and Victory Boulevard and the Staten Island landfill on the others, there's a short self-guided trail walk here, as well as a creek that's popular with local canoeists. The trail entrance is on Travis Avenue; call the Greenbelt office at 718-667-2165 for travel directions.

Closer to the ferry terminal is an eight-acre gem of a zoo that's run by the Staten Island Zoological Society. On the grounds of a former private estate off Forest Avenue (take the S-48 bus), it opened in 1936 as the country's first educational zoo. An estimated 100,000 schoolchildren visit here each year, drawn by the children's zoo's collection of farm animals grazing in a New England–style farm setting, on the other side of an authentic covered bridge. There's an Animal Hospital and Nursery, too, not to mention outdoor attractions like a pony barn and track, a flamingo pool, and a "town" of playful prairie dogs. In the main building, one of two wings has been transformed into a realistic tropical forest traversed by a wooden boardwalk. The other, to be completed by 1994, will represent an African savannah at twilight. The pièce de resistance here, however, may be the serpentarium, which contains more rattlesnakes than an Indiana Jones movie. Call 718-442-3100.

The Indians called it Narriockh. Dutch colonists named it Conyme Eyland, presumably after the conies, or wild rabbits, that bounded across its sandy dunes. For the past thirty-five years or so, Coney Island–Brooklyn's atmospherically down-at-the-heels center for fun in the sun—has been home to the New York Aquarium, now the Aquarium for Wildlife Conservation. Overlooking the boardwalk which has bordered Coney Island's six-mile stretch of beach since 1921, the aquarium is also the official residence of more than 10,000 aquatic life-forms: from giant Japanese spider crabs to dolphins, sea lions, and Nuka, one of New York's only two Pacific walruses.

Walk through the entrance and marvel at below-water views of beluga whales cavorting in the 180,000-gallon Oceanic Tank. Striped bass, sea robins, and flounders snagged by local fishermen are on display at the native sea-life exhibit; a cold-water tank in Discovery Cove has creepy-looking wolf eels, giant spider crabs, and an even bigger octopus. Sharks with dead-button eyes glide malevolently through the waters of a 90,000-gallon tank that holds the safe from the *Andrea Doria,* which sank off the coast of Nantucket. But the newest crowd-pleaser is the 300-foot-long simulated piece of rocky coastline that runs parallel to the boardwalk. Called Sea Cliffs, it's not only a realistic habitat for California sea otters and a herd of friendly harbor seals—seen via an indoor corridor with underwater views—but also home to Nuka and Tiipaq, two hefty Pacific walruses with an equally large following of pint-sized human fans. The aquarium's telephone number is 718-265-FISH.

Sometime in late 1993, when the old Prospect Park Zoo reopens as Brooklyn's new Prospect Park Wildlife Center, a five-year-long, $30 million renovation will have transformed another dreary urban animal jail into a nine-acre interactive children's zoo made up of naturalistic open spaces. A kid-size prarie dog burrow has been specially designed to allow kids an up-close view of a prairie-dog town. Baboons will run freer than usual in a transplanted savannah; parakeets will fly through an Australian grassland; various lucky jungle fowl will have their own forest floor to forage in; and a pole barn in the pasture area will be home to a variety of pettable domestic farm animals. To find out more, call 718-399-7333.

A "working farm" with domestic rabbits, ponies, goats, and sheep is also a highlight of the Queens Zoo/Wildlife Center, at least for kids. Queens has had its own zoo since 1968, when the previous incarnation opened on the site of the 1964 World's Fair in Flushing Meadows. The newly expanded and renovated conservation center's emphasis on North America's wildlife and woodlands is an added pleasure, however—especially if you're already in the neighborhood to sight-see some of Flushing's historic "Freedom Mile" attractions.

From the entrance at 111th Street and 54th Avenue, follow the user-friendly system of pathways that travels around the eleven-acre zoo's perimeter, pausing at bridges and viewing platforms along the way. You'll see black bears lumbering beneath a scenic waterfall; a flock of wild turkeys; a highly populated prairie-dog village; and a tree-shaded, three-acre range where a herd of American bison wander comparatively free. Coyotes, say officials, are making a comeback in New York state, and a few of them live here, just past the sea-lion exhibit. A herd of imposing Roosevelt elk—native to the mountains and forests of western states—can be observed from a nearby overlook. Pumas and bobcats are on the prowl around the next bend, but first stop in at the geodesic dome. Designed by Buckminster Fuller for the World's Fair, it's been transformed into a marvelous, airy aviary that rises from lushly planted forest floor to the tops of trees—and is filled with blue-wing teal ducks, magpies, cattle egret, cardinals, and various other species. Sandhill cranes, one of only two native North American cranes, have an outdoor oasis all their own, next to a man-made marshland inhabited by herons, egrets, migrating geese, and other wild birds. Call 718-271-7761 for hours and directions.

The parklands of Queens—from forest to seashore—are already a birders' paradise, especially during the migratory rush hours of spring and fall. In Forest Park, more than thirty types of warblers have been spotted in a single day, and black-crowned night herons can be found year-round in Alley Pond Park. One of the best parts of the city to spot migrating kestrel, tree swallows, and monarch butterflies is the barrier beach at Jacob Riis Park. Every summer, usually at the end of August—the height of the butterflies' arduous journey from Canada to Mexico—free butterfly migration tours are offered at the nearby Jamaica Bay Wildlife Refuge, another part of the Gateway National Recreation Area. Better yet, take an afternoon off and visit the wildlife refuge any time of year. This is one of the country's greatest urban nature escapes: over 9,000 acres of tidal wetlands, fields, salt marsh, and woods perched in the middle of Jamaica Bay, not far from the runways of JFK International Airport.

It's about a mile down Cross Bay Boulevard from the Broad Channel subway station (A or CC on the IND line) to the low, modern brick building that houses the visitor center. Stop in for a pass—they're free, and, if you come back a second time, you're awarded a permanent refuge permit. You can also pick up trail maps; find out about year-round nature walks, birding workshops, and other programs; or duck into the adjacent education hall where tanks of diamondback terrapins, hermit crabs, and webbed-footed turtles are on display and wildlife lectures take place during part of the year.

Over 330 different species of birds have been spotted in the refuge since it was created in the early 1950s (by digging man-made ponds and dikes and planting beach grass, trees, and other vegetation to enhance the original salt marsh). Among them are the occasional eagles, plus terns, common barn swallows, woodcocks, and cardinals. Snowy egrets and glossy ibis nest here by the hundreds, waterfowl fly in for the milder winters, and a few years ago a pair of ospreys hatched two fledglings on one of the refuge's specially constructed nesting platforms, marking the first successful osprey nesting in the city in a century. "Birds are the most obvious form of wildlife," National Park Ranger Kathy Krause, a New York City native, tells me. "But we manage other kinds, too." Including frogs, painted turtles, several species of snakes, muskrats, raccoons, chipmunks, and (at least) sixty colorful varieties of butterflies, drawn by the nectar-providing flowers and shrubs specially planted to attract them.

On the other side of Cross Bay Boulevard, the East Pond Trail curves through marsh, grassland, shrubbery, and (sometimes) mud, especially in late summer, when the water level is lowered to provide additional mudflats for migrating shorebirds. The shorter, sandier West Pond Trail leads from woods and grasslands to a one-time tern nesting area where native bay turtles now lay their eggs (in late May and early June). Or follow the signs for the Upland Trail, which starts just past a box marked "Bird Log" by the visitor center's back door. Wide and gravelled at the start, farther on edged by tangled, overgrown shrubbery and thickets of coralberries that turn a brilliant red in autumn, clusters of salt-spray roses begin to bloom along here in May. There's a grove of fragrant red cedar trees, not far from the north garden area's evergreen, holly, and bamboolike reed grass; in winter, you might even spot a long-eared owl roosting in a thick grove of Japanese pines.

For information about walks, wildlife lectures, and other programs at the Jamaica Bay Wildlife Refuge, call 718-318-4340 or write to Gateway NRA Wildlife Refuge District, Floyd Bennett Field, Brooklyn, NY 11234.

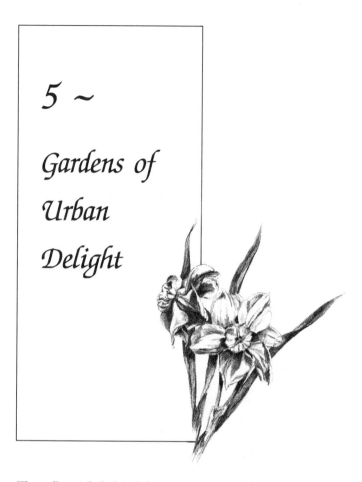

5 ~

Gardens of Urban Delight

They flourish behind brownstones on the Upper East Side, bloom next to churches in the West Village, proliferate in public parks in Brooklyn, Queens, and the Bronx. Look up when you're walking around midtown Manhattan and you'll see them on rooftops, in towering glass-walled atriums, or, at street level, squeezed into postage-stamp-size spaces between adjoining buildings. Whatever their size, the gardens of New York offer respite from the madding crowd around you, even a moment's treasured solitude.

Some are old: Fifth Avenue's Rockefeller Center—which one landmark guide calls the "village green of modern New

York"—was the site of the city's first botanical garden back in the early 1800s; the memory survives in the Channel Gardens' seasonal plantings and annual flower show. Others, like Bryant Park behind the New York Public Library at Fifth Avenue and 42nd Street, are newly improved. A multimillion-dollar restoration has transformed this former drug dealers' haven into four acres of grassy lawn and carefully tended plots of flower beds. Concerts are held here in spring and summer, and there's a TKTS booth that sells discounted tickets for city-wide music and dance events. Several postage-stamp-size "pocket parks" are also in the midtown area, including Greenacre Park on 51st Street between Second and Third avenues. On weekday mornings, people rushing by on their way to work gaze in enviously: Well-dressed business-people are leisurely reading the *Times* next to the cascading waterfall and elderly couples, perched by planters of shrubbery and flowers, peacefully sip cups of tea or coffee purchased from the adjacent snack bar. In fall, the golden leaves of thornless honey locust trees cover the park's brick terrace like damp, oval pieces-of-eight.

For temporary shelter on Madison Avenue, try the indoor IBM Garden Plaza at 56th Street, which is filled with green bamboo trees, round ceramic bowls planted with an array of color-coordinated flowers, and tourists studying sightseeing maps. Off Third Avenue, the Ford Foundation building on 42nd Street is one of the city's original indoor atriums, where you can walk down steps to a sunken pool edged by thick clusters of lilies and pine trees. Less than a block east, the United Nations has its own share of greenery: Walkways and lawns stretch north along First Avenue from 42nd to 48th streets, offering photogenic views of the 59th Street Bridge and Roosevelt Island. In spring, thousands of daffodils explode in a vibrant burst of yellow; in summer, the scent of garden roses gamely competes with exhaust fumes from the FDR Drive.

Culture blooms year-round in the city's museums, which also boast gardenlike spaces with their own artistic merit. The Museum of Modern Art, on West 53rd Street between Fifth and Sixth, has a sculpture garden that feeds the soul, a café that feeds the body—and evening "SummerGarden" concerts that highlight the works of a different composer each year; call 212-708-9480. The Metropolitan Museum of Art, on Fifth Avenue at 82nd Street, has a Chinese scholar's garden as well as grander installments like the skylit Temple of Dendur. Special exhibitions and lectures are held (in season) in an open-air setting on the Roof Garden, planted with pansies, honeysuckle vines and wisteria. On weekends, when the museum stays open late, it's a perfect perch for watching the sun set over Central Park. For information, call 212-535-7710.

The city's only Tibetan museum, set on a steep hillside in an upscale suburban neighborhood of Staten Island, was founded in 1945 by a woman named Jacques Marchais who, though she never visited Tibet herself, was fascinated enough by the country and culture to build a monastic-style stone building to house her rich collection of Tibetan religious art, which includes twenty or thirty Buddhas carefully arranged on a three-tiered altar backed by scroll-like thanka paintings.

Prayer flags drift in the breeze of the adjacent garden, which, though small, has a carefully orchestrated serenity. There's a pond scattered with lily pads (while I was there, a black-and-white cat dreamily watched unwary orange carp circling around), and various pint-size animal sculptures are scattered throughout. On a hot summer afternoon it's cool and restful, the muted blare of traffic barely audible through surrounding foliage. For directions, call 718-987-3500.

In the West Village, head for St. Luke's-in-the-Fields, a red brick chapel at the corner of Hudson and Grove streets that belongs to downtown Manhattan's Trinity Parish.

Courtyard garden at the Cloisters, Fort Tryon Park

Built in 1821, when the Village was a rural retreat from the burgeoning metropolis south of Canal, it has an even tinier hidden garden with benches ideal for passing time with a book or a friend. A couple of fearless Beatrix Potter–like squirrels—one gray and one black—kept me company on a recent visit. Or trek (by IND subway) north to Fort Tryon Park, where the Cloisters sits high above the rest of the city like a surreal vision of fifteenth-century France with excellent views of the Hudson. Much of this castlelike blend of ancient French monastic arcades and columns was imported and reconstructed here, stone by ancient stone. The result is inspiring—both inside, where the Metropolitan Museum of Art's collection of tapestries and rare illuminated manuscripts provides the perfect setting for a series of appropriately medieval lectures and concerts—and out, where gardens of the Middle Ages have been lovingly recreated.

Chamomile, lavender, and pennyroyal grow in the Bonnefont Cloister herb garden; the adjacent Trie Cloister garden is a live re-creation of the primroses, wild strawberries, and plants featured in the museum's famed Unicorn Tapestries. And in the Cuxa Cloister's Garth Garden, you can sit on a bench beneath colonnaded walkways, listening to the tranquil splash of water from the central fountain. Tours are offered in May and June, and again in September and October; call 212-923-3700.

Central Park's Conservatory Garden not only looks like the grounds of an English manor or a French château. The park's only formal garden—between 103d and 106th streets— is also far enough from midtown to keep most visitors to the city from discovering its fountains, lilac trees, and peaceful paths lined by hedges, flower beds, and benches from the 1939 World's Fair.

The iron gate at Fifth Avenue and 105th Street once led to Cornelius Vanderbilt's mansion on 58th Street, but now it guards steps that lead into the Central Garden, a favorite spot for spring and summer wedding photographs. There are three gardens in all—North, South, and Central—each with its own fountain. The South, or "secret garden," has a particularly romantic charm: Snapdragons spill over onto the path in the fall; holly bushes and other perennials provide greenery even in January. There are tours on Saturdays through mid-November.

When the screech of brakes and the squeal of tires is overwhelming, pocket parks and indoor atriums provide a quick shot of tranquility. A visit to the city's major botanical gardens, on the other hand, are the equivalent of a mega-dose of tranquilizers—and the granddaddy of them all is the New York Botanical Garden. Though located in the Bronx, it's easy to get to: Metro North (Harlem Line) trains from Grand Central bring you close to the entrance; there's also a weekend bus service that picks up passengers from the Metropolitan Museum of Art and the Museum of Natural History.

Admission to this 250-acre "nature museum," founded in 1895 by Cornelius Vanderbilt, Andrew Carnegie, J. Pierpont Morgan, and Nathanial Lord Britton (a professor of botany at Columbia University), is on a pay-what-you-wish basis. There's also a (very) minimal fee to enter two of the sixteen specialty gardens scattered around the landscaped grounds as well as to explore the Enid Haupt Conservatory, a nineteenth-century glass palace where you'll find humid rain forests, English spring flowers, and arid desert landscapes. (Note: The Conservatory reopens in the spring of 1995.)

Miles of paths wind around the five demonstration gardens, the Rock Garden, and through the maze of the Children's Garden. You could cover it all in about an hour or two, but why rush? Stop and smell the roses in the Rose Garden. Better yet, take your time ambling along the trails that wind through the forty-acre forest—jutted with glacier rocks and

New York Botanical Garden

dark with hemlock, beech, and red oak—which grows on both sides of the Bronx River. It's a remnant of New York's original wilderness. The river spills over a six-foot dam near an old snuff mill, now an informal snack bar/restaurant. Then walk back along Azalea Way—one of the Botanical Garden's "main" thoroughfares—to the Visitor Information Center (718-817-8705) and gift shop, both housed in a majestic limestone mansion.

The Queens Botanical Garden has flowered on a thirty-eight-acre plot of land between Main Street and College Point Boulevard since 1963, not far from its original twenty-acre site in adjacent Flushing Meadow Park (where it overgrew from a five-acre display created for the 1939 New York World's Fair). The garden's three-acre Victorian Wedding Garden, where a willow tree droops gracefully over a small stream, is as romantic as it sounds (more than 10,000 couples have tied the knot here). By far the most spectacular display, if you don't count springtime's 80,000 tulips, is the Charles H. Perkins Memorial Rose Garden, where every possible shape, size, and color are displayed on six acres that make up the largest rose garden in the northeastern United States. By June the scent is ambrosial. (Take the IRT Flushing Line #7 train to Main Street, then the Q-44 bus to the garden.) Call 718-886-3800 for hours and special events.

Since opening at the edge of Prospect Park in 1910, the Brooklyn Botanic Garden has offered city-dwellers a glimpse of nature at its best. The Cherry Esplanade's seventy-six Japanese cherry trees perfume the air starting in late March; a little later, so do the masses of azaleas, crabapples, and wisteria that dress up the garden's formal, Italian-style Osborne Section.

In full bloom during summer, the Cranford Rose Garden recently won an award from the Garden Club of America for "unusual rose collections of special merit." And if a storm blows up, you can always retreat to the white-columned Steinhardt Conservatory, which houses tropical, warm temperate, and desert pavilions. Before leaving, marvel at the country's oldest collection of dwarf bonsai trees on display in the Bonsai Museum or weather the storm in the Japanese Garden, where a pond, graceful bridges, and a 500-year-old Shogun lantern are combined with Zen-like landscaping as lovely when the weather's fine as when it's not. (Occasionally, contributions are suggested before entering.) Call 718-622-4433 for directions and more information.

Snug Harbor Cultural Center has been home to the Staten Island Botanical Garden since 1977, which means you can admire the metropolitan area's largest English Perennial Garden here, as well as a greenhouse that houses a collection of more than 116 rare Amazonian and Caribbean orchids.

You can also stroll down woodland trails, picnic on rolling lawns, feed the ducks at a natural pond—and while you're at it, visit an avant-garde museum, an outstanding children's museum, or enjoy a wide array of concerts and performances. The fact that few Manhattanites seem to know about this unique urban cultural park a short (S-40) bus ride away from the Staten Island ferry terminal makes it even more appealing. Neighborhood residents, on the other hand, long ago turned it into an informal dog-walking club. "I knew all the dogs' names before I knew the people," says one of the six Snug Harbor Rangers who patrols the eighty-three-acre grounds, and who reports that wildlife living near the marshy lower pond includes egrets, snapping turtles, wild ducks, and pheasants.

"If you put Wolf Trap into Colonial Williamsburg," a volunteer tells me, "you'd come out with Snug Harbor." The colonial part may be an exaggeration (after all, Snug Harbor wasn't founded as a home for retired sailors until 1831), but the Wolf Trap analogy isn't too far off. There's a regular series of musical events here, ranging from Philharmonic concerts on the South Meadow to performances by local country western bands at a gazebo close to the Visitors Center (718-448-2500). Pick up a self-guided tour map and other useful information at the desk, have a coffee and a sandwich at Melville's Cafe, browse through the gift shop, and stop for a minute to read the wall displays, which show and tell the history of the place. At one point, more than a thousand old salts lived here—and, as an excerpt from a book by Theodore Dreiser puts it, "Not a few of them are given to swearing loudly, drinking frequently, snoring heavily on Sundays and otherwise disporting themselves in droll and unsanctified ways."

In winter, or summer when there's a downpour, concerts take place at the nearby Veterans' Hall, a former seamen's chapel that's been cushily transformed into a comfortable small venue. In the middle of the stately row of templelike Greek Revival mansions that face the waters of the Kill Van Kull, you'll find the old Main Hall, now the Newhouse Center for Contemporary Art. The floor is inlaid with nautical compass points, cobalt-blue windows on the second floor are stenciled with different constellations, and stained-glass pictures of steamships, lighthouses, and other nautical themes are set in transoms above the doorways. Originally a community gallery and exhibition space, this has grown to become one of the city's most interesting museums. "The whole island is like a garden," wrote Henry David Thoreau, after spending a summer not far from here in 1843. And though this isn't a garden in the traditional sense, it does represent a nurturing of lesser-known artistic talent well worth an hour or so's exploration.

The most peaceful garden of all might be the one that's permanent home to the remains of over 300,000 New Yorkers,

Veterans' Memorial Hall, Snug Harbor

including five former mayors, Herman Melville, Bat Masterson, George M. Cohan, and Duke Ellington. Like Brooklyn's Greenwood, the Bronx's Woodlawn Cemetery has also been a weirdly popular tourist attraction for more than a century. Only half an hour by train from Grand Central to the Woodlawn station, it's just a short walk from there to the main office at the corner of 233d Street and Webster Avenue, where you can pick up a map that guides you through the cemetery's miles of paths. Monuments, mausoleums, and gravestones, from simple to grandiose and sculptured, grace 400 acres of landscaped hills and streams, and almost 200 kinds of birds have been spotted, attracted by the majestic pine, linden, beech, and other trees old, large, or important enough to be included in a list of "Great Trees of New York."

Created to honor the dead, Woodlawn's idyllic setting just as easily lends itself to artistic endeavors of the living; the cemetery is the frequent site of outdoor sculpture exhibits cosponsored by the Bronx Council of the Arts. (A recent show was titled, appropriately, "Houses of Spirit/Memories of Ancestors.") The city may have exploded around what was—when it opened in 1863—a remote rural sanctuary, but enough country atmosphere is left to make an afternoon here a strangely reviving experience. For more information, call 718-920-0500.

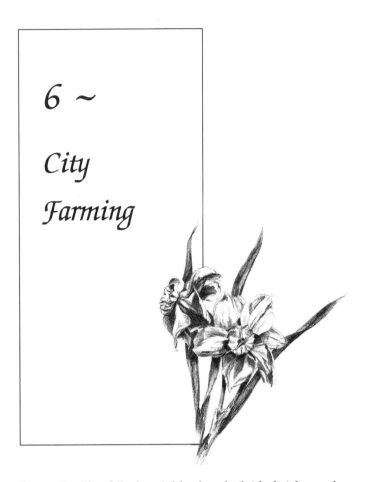

6 ~

City
Farming

In a quiet Floral Park neighborhood of tidy brick row houses and apartment buildings, the old white farmhouse looks out of place at first—as if you'd taken a wrong turn somewhere on the Long Island Expressway and accidentally stumbled onto a patch of New England. In fact, the Queens County Farm Museum is New York City's only official working farm, a forty-seven-acre vestige of the days when the northeastern corner of Queens was barely settled wilderness and your closest neighbors lived miles away, not right next door.

If you crave a day in the country but don't feel like leaving the city, this is the next best thing. A narrow dirt drive leads down to a seven-acre farmyard filled with geese, sheep, cows, and pigs. Homegrown fruits and vegetables are for sale (in season) at a small stand just inside the entrance, and you can enjoy hayrides, nature trails, crafts fairs, an antique auto show, even a "spring fling" complete with Maypoles and Morris dancers. In summer, the annual Thunderbird American Indian Pow Wow takes place here, followed by the Queens County Fair in September and an October apple festival that stars the world's largest apple cobbler.

A farmer named Jacob Adriance built the Flemish-style house in 1772 (his grandfather, Elbert Adriance, bought the land in 1697). Doubled in size between 1833 and 1840, the house includes the original kitchen where crocks and pewter plates line the mantel above an open hearth. Rustic pottery and other vintage implements are stacked carefully on shelves—along with a few subtle, modern touches like a bowl of Sunkist oranges and some noncolonial cleaning stuff by the sink.

Your average nineteenth-century housewife would have delighted in the kitchen garden, planted with herbs and vegetables handy for picking at a moment's notice. She'd probably be impressed with the present-day farm's rather luxurious chicken coop, too, which dates from the 1920s and comes with a view of surrounding apple orchards. In the cow shed, Daisy, a mild-mannered Ayrshire, lives in pungent harmony with a couple of sheep, a few goats, and a black-faced ram donated by a traveling farm exhibit; at last count, the farm's other livestock included twenty ducks, eight geese, a few peacocks, and a pair of plump, messy pigs named Laverne and Shirley. On weekends, there's a free tour of the farmhouse—or stop in for a second to pick up one of the visitors' maps and self-guided tour brochures. They're stacked next to the "eggs for sale" sign, on a table just inside the door. For directions call 718-347-FARM.

Prospect Park Meadow's Port Arch

In Brooklyn's Prospect Park, the Lefferts Homestead is one of the borough's few surviving seventeenth- and eighteenth-century Dutch farmhouses (call the Brooklyn Historical Society at 718-624-0890 to find out about occasional tours to some of the others). Dating back to 1783, the white clapboard house was built by a prominent Flatbush resident named Peter Lefferts on the foundations of an earlier structure destroyed during the Revolutionary War.

A few of the Lefferts family's original possessions, including a grandfather clock and a four-poster bed, as well as spinning wheels and antique toys, are displayed in roped-off period rooms. There's also a regular series of family-oriented workshops and special events, including exhibits on quilt-making and other early American crafts, plus an annual Harvest Fair in October. Because of its location—between the Prospect Park carousel and zoo—the museum's focus is understandably on activities for children, with hands-on, interactive exhibits that help them imagine what it might be like to live back in 1820 or so. Call 718-965-6505.

The city's oldest farmhouse, as well as its first officially designated landmark, is in Brooklyn's Flatlands district. Built in 1652 by Pieter Claesen Wyckoff, an indentured servant who ultimately became one of the settlement's most prosperous citizens, the small, simple house lay in the heart of a large farm carved from salt marsh that originally belonged to the Carnarsie Indians. Today, the Pieter Claesen Wyckoff House Museum is set in a one-and-a-half-acre park planted with the kind of greenery the Wyckoff family might find familiar: a kitchen garden with vegetables and herbs in easy reach, a bulb garden with more than a thousand spring-blooming daffodils and tulips.

In a particularly nice touch, visitors are encouraged to pick—and take home—some of the kitchen garden's seasonal plantings, an informal approach that extends to the house itself, where rooms feature a mix of period furniture open to close-up observation. Craft workshops in flax and wool spinning, butter- and cheese-making, weaving, and concerts of eighteenth-century music take place on a regular basis. So do special events, including a St. Nicholas Day Celebration during which St. Nick arrives, Dutch-style, on a white horse instead of by sleigh. A small exhibition space is used for two rotating displays, one on the restoration of the house, the other a selection of historic objects and documents culled from the museum's permanent collection. Call 718-629-5400 for the best way to get there.

It's easy to miss the small plaque on the north side of the apartment building at 16 Park Avenue. "This marks the geographic center of the farm known in Revolutionary Days as 'Inclenberg,' " it reads, "owned by Robert Murray, whose wife, Mary Lindley Murray . . . rendered signal service in the Revolutionary War."

The farm disappeared centuries ago, but the Murrays' name still lives on in Murray Hill, the midtown neighborhood that stretches east of Madison Avenue. One of several reminders of the days when much of the city was farmland. Another lies a few miles north, where Manhattan's sole remaining intact Dutch colonial farmhouse stands in a pocket of colonial-type trees and flowers at 204th and Broadway—a wood-and-fieldstone relic from the past adrift in an asphalt-and-concrete present. Constructed in 1784, when Broadway was an unpaved dirt road, the sloped-roof Dyckman House was then the center of one of New York's largest landholdings, famed for its cherry and apple orchards, and later, as grazing pasture for cattle. (Dyckman Street, which joins the Harlem River Drive with the Henry Hudson Parkway and divides Fort Tryon Park from Inwood Hill Park, is further proof of the family's prominence.)

What's left includes a tiny, fenced-in garden of heirloom vegetables and herbs, along with a still-blooming descendant of the Dyckmans' cherry trees. Twisted wisteria boughs frame the entrance to the house, where a low-ceilinged parlor and dining room are furnished in such true eighteenth- and nineteenth-century fashion that you half expect to see the widow of statesman Alexander Hamilton drop in for tea and free advice from Jacobus Dyckman, a respected local judge whose father, William Dyckman, built the house. Succeeding generations of the Dyckman family lived here until 1855 or so; in one of two upstairs bedrooms you'll even find the cradle that rocked numerous Dyckman infants.

Down a flight of steep stairs, the kitchen's open hearth and spinning wheel offer a look at what housewives coped with before the advent of modern conveniences. The nearby Relic Room's Revolutionary War artifacts—a blue broadcloth general's uniform, a couple of musket bullets as big as marbles—are a reminder that, during the War of Independence, northern Manhattan was occupied by British troops and Hessian mercenaries. The reconstructed Hessian soldier's hut, an authentically dank and sour-smelling relic in back of the house, is another. For more information, call 212-304-9422.

Jacobus Dyckman, who ran a small tavern on the Manhattan side of Spuyten Duyvil before becoming a judge, was one of several prominent local citizens who helped finance a "farmers' bridge" across the creek, eliminating the need for them to pay the King's Bridge toll between Manhattan and the Bronx. The tolls are even higher these days, but farmers from Long Island, upstate New York, New Jersey, and farther afield still truck their produce across various bridges and into various parts of the city. One destination is the year-round, indoor Jamaica Farmers' Market in Queens (90–40 160th Street, 718-291-0282), a half block north of Jamaica Avenue, the first full-time indoor farmers' market to open in New York since the 1930s.

Another stop is any of the city's Greenmarkets—about eighteen at last count. By far the largest, with over sixty vendors, is held Saturdays year-round in Union Square Park, at 17th Street and Broadway. In the 1700s, this land was part of a farm belonging to the well-off Breevort family, who owned most of Manhattan from here down to 8th Street. Later used as a Civil War parade ground and still later as the site of protests against everything from the 1927 executions of Sacco and Vanzetti to the massive unemployment of the 1930s, today the Greenmarket site on the park's northern boundary is piled with so many varieties of fruits and vegetables that, as one farmer remarked, "it's getting so we have to go to New York to buy our own produce." Arrive early enough and you'll see them unloading (in summer) more kinds of lettuce, apples, tomatoes, squash, and herbs than you knew existed. In winter, it's the best place in town for homemade jams and jellies, maple syrup, and steaming cups of hot apple cider. "I couldn't exist without it," admits an Upper West Side woman on her way to catch the subway uptown, arms filled with bags of potatoes, onions, dried flowers, and various esoteric greens.

Not far away, there's a summer Greenmarket outside St. Mark's Church on Second Avenue and 10th Street—the site of early New Amsterdam governor "Peg Leg" Peter Stuyvesant's family "bouwerie," or farm. Another operates from the school-yard at PS 41, on Greenwich Avenue in the West Village, while others are scattered throughout Manhattan, Brooklyn, and the Bronx. For a complete list of locations and times, or information about tours of the Union Square Greenmarket, call 212-477-3220 or drop by the green-and-white Greenmarket booth at Union Square on Monday, Wednesday, Friday or Saturday.

When most of New York was farmland, the closest farmers' market was your own backyard. Today, Operation GreenThumb, the country's largest municipally run community gardening program, helps local communities transform rubble-filled vacant lots into minifarms that, recently, produced a million dollars' worth of city-grown fruits and vegetables in a single year. The best place to see the results for yourself is at the annual City Gardeners' Harvest Fair, which takes place at Brooklyn's Floyd Bennett Field each August and fills the air with the smell of livestock and maple-sugar candy.

At one booth, you might find a clutch of eager 4-H Club members from Bedford-Stuyvesant busily hawking T-shirts, at another, an elderly Brooklyn lady selling pone cake made from local zucchinis. "Someone changed my sign to read 'Pound Cake,' " she tells me with a laugh. "I kept trying to tell them it really is pone cake." Nearby, what looks like miles of tomatoes, green peppers, eggplants, lettuce, and other vegetables are displayed on tables that stretch from one end of the old airport's hangar to the other—entries in a blue–ribbon winning contest as good as any you'd find in Iowa.

Long before there were farms, before there was a city even, Native Americans lived on the abundant game and wild foods of the area. Remarkably, New York still sustains all sorts of indigenous foods. To find out where they grow, however, you'd have to ask "Wildman" Steve Brill, a forty-four-year-old Queens native and self-taught naturalist and field botanist who since 1982 has conducted "foraging tours" of parks in all five boroughs (to book one, call 718-291-6825). Employed by the parks department at one point, his career in wild foods started when he was searching for exotic natural ingredients to cook with—and with the help of field guides, discovered hundreds of locations where edible berries, vegetables, seeds, mushrooms, seaweeds, and herbs could be harvested. Recent discoveries have included a persimmon tree in Central Park (north of the Ramble) and a wild potato vine in Inwood Hill Park. The Old Motor Parkway passing through Alley Pond Park, he says, is a virtual treasure trove of wild foods, including blackberries, jerusalem artichokes, and shaggy parasol mushrooms that grow in the piles of lawn clippings casually dumped by local residents. Wild cherries, raspberries, hedge mustard, curly dock, and the ubiquitous oyster mushroom, which even grows on neighborhood trees, are a few of the other wild foods he's found throughout the city. "I don't have a favorite park," Brill says. "I consider the whole ecosystem as one unit with different sections, that just happens to have buildings and people in between."

Farm Trips

The idea is to increase understanding between the city and nearby farming communities. To help achieve that goal, FarmHands-CityHands organizes farm-food tastings and "country summer evenings" at local restaurants (like the Hudson River Club), sends New Yorkers to work on regional farms, and offers FarmDay field trips that combine history and tradition, often with a cram course in regional cuisine and culture. Recent journeys have taken city-dwellers to an Eastern Woodland Indians' longhouse in Connecticut, an eighteenth-century manor house and farm on the Hudson, a pre-Revolutionary inn, and a commercial apple orchard in upstate New York. Tours generally leave from the Greenmarkets at Union Square and Columbus Avenue. Prices average from $35 to $85; less for members (who also receive discounts at participating area wineries, farmstands, and farm bed and breakfasts). For information, call or write FarmHands-Cityhands, 34 Downing St., New York, NY 10014, 212-627-HAND.

The New York State Guide to Farm Fresh Food (Metro Region) includes "pick-your-own" farms as well as farms that offer tours to groups and individuals. For a free copy, write to the State of New York Department of Agriculture and Markets, 1 Winners Circle, Albany, NY 12235.

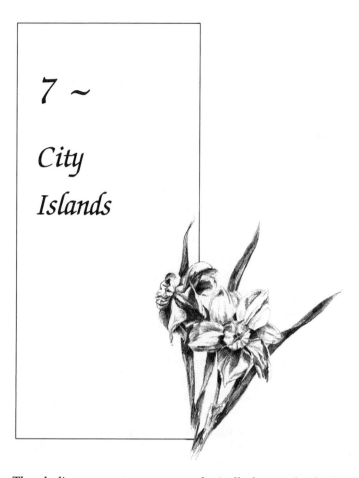

7 ~

City
Islands

The skyline seems to grow paradoxically larger the farther it recedes; by the time the ferry is parallel with the Statue of Liberty, lower Manhattan's multilevel blocks of gleaming glass have turned into the kind of picture-perfect view that has Italian lovers, French honeymooners, and British tourists cooing and clutching their cameras.

"Whadzat white stuff, Dad?" asks a boy of six or seven who, Mets cap pulled low on his forehead, is staring raptly at the ferry's foamy wake. When his dad explains it's salt, the kid looks as skeptical as if he'd been told it was vanilla ice cream.

Even New Yorkers can forget they're living in a seafaring metropolis, surrounded by water on almost all sides. A trip aboard the Staten Island Ferry—especially on a clear, windy day when the sky's as blue as a Colorado morning—is not only the cheapest way to view the country's most celebrated monument up close, it's also a reminder that, while Manhattan is the most famous island, Brooklyn, like Queens, is technically on Long Island, that forked peninsula that stretches east from the city's two major airports, and only the Bronx can truly claim to be part of the mainland.

The city's third largest borough (formerly the Borough of Richmond), Staten Island is far enough from the rest of the city that, in recent years, a secessionist movement has sprung up that advocates everything from joining New Jersey to a tongue-in-cheek suggestion that it become an independent republic. According to one bit of apocryphal lore, a seventeenth-century ship race resulted in Staten Island becoming part of New York in the first place. Both New Jersey (then known poetically as Nova Cesarea) and New York claimed it. So in 1688, the Duke of York—whose brother, King Charles II, had granted him the newly British colony to govern twenty years earlier—decreed that the island would belong to whoever could sail around its circumference in twenty-four hours or less.

A sea captain named Christopher Billop took up the challenge, succeeding in an hour under the allotted time. Staten Island, so the story goes, has been part of New York ever since. However, transportation to Manhattan was erratic until more than a century later, when "Commodore" Cornelius Vanderbilt, then an enterprising teenager (later one of the country's richest men) first began offering windjammer, then steamboat passenger service. Today's ferries follow the same route, plying New York Harbor between the terminal in lower

Manhattan and the town of St. George on Staten Island, with thousands of regular commuters and almost uncountable numbers of tourists going along for the twenty-five-minute ride, which not only includes an incomparable view of Lady Liberty but passes close enough to Ellis Island for you (almost) to count the windows of the Museum of Immigration. (For departure times, call 718-727-2508.)

There's a ten-minute turnaround wait on weekends, which barely gives you time to check out the tiny Staten Island Ferry Maritime Museum (recently renamed the Staten Island Ferry Collection) that's conveniently located—along with a branch of McDonald's and other fast-food outlets, phones, and rest rooms—in the terminal on Staten Island. Or take a walk to Richmond Terrace, a waterside street where a funky weekly Saturday fair takes place from 10:00 A.M. to dusk: various local artists, artisans, and other vendors are on hand with a wide variety of crafts and food for sale. The Staten Island Institute of Arts and Sciences (75 Stuyvesant Place, telephone 718-727-1135), which also operates the Ferry Collection, is housed in a stately Georgian Revival building a short walk from the ferry pier; it's well worth browsing through its three special exhibition galleries and permanent displays of local natural history, art, furniture, costumes, and other artifacts from the island's last hundred years or so.

Until recently, the Staten Island ferry only cost 25 cents; it's still a bargain at 50 cents (deposit two quarters into the turnstile for the return trip). Especially when you consider that a ticket for the Statue of Liberty ferry, which also departs from Battery Park, is a lot more (as of this writing, $6.00 for adults and $3.00 for children 12 and under). A national monument since 1933, the statue stands majestically on Liberty Island, which, in New York's early days, belonged to a French immigrant named Isaac Bedloe. It was still known as Bedloe's Island on July 4th, 1884, when Frederic Auguste Bartholdi, an ambitious and idealistic French sculptor, presented his 151-foot-high colossus to the city as an enduring symbol of French-American friendship.

Bartholdi, whose vision is said to have been inspired by the great pyramids of Egypt, was assisted by his countryman Alexandre Gustave Eiffel, the famed engineer who a few years later built the tower in Paris that bears his name. Weighing in at over 225 tons, *Liberty Enlightening the World* (the statue's official name) attracts over a million visitors a year. If you're up to it, nothing can beat the experience of climbing up the dizzying interior stairway to admire the panoramic view from the observation platform in the statue's crown. On the other hand, there's a perfectly good observation deck near the base.

Tickets for the ferry are sold at Castle Clinton, the reddish stone fort—and national historic monument—that stands at the southern tip of Battery Park and that once guarded the city from a point about 200 yards offshore. You can also buy tickets here for the even more expensive trip to Ellis Island, also known as the Island of Tears. Over half the immigrants who came to this country between 1892 and 1924 passed through its gates; today, the somber, red brick buildings contain a heart-wrenching collection of archival photographs and tape-recorded personal recollections that make for a sobering, as well as fascinating, experience.

Plan on at least an hour in line for either ferry, particularly in good weather when the crowd represents one of the more diverse slices of world culture to be found anywhere: Dashikied families from Africa, somberly attired Amish families from Pennsylvania, cowboy-hatted Texans all patiently waiting their turn. (Free entertainment is sometimes provided by local street performers, including an occasional skateboarding daredevil leaping over garbage bins.) For departure times, call 212-269-5755.

Next to the cavernous Staten Island ferry terminal—a nondescript building which may soon be transformed into an imaginative modern facility complete with shops, restaurants, and a giant clock visible from the water—the slightly decrepit structure on South Street is the Battery Maritime Building, from which the ferry for Governors Island departs. Site of a brief, early Dutch settlement, the 173-acre island has served as a military stronghold since the days when British men-of-war patrolled the harbor; in 1966, the Coast Guard took over. Although it is not usually accessible to the public, you can admire the island's eighteenth-century fort and picnic on lawns that stretch down to the water during the annual one-day open house held (usually) at the end of June. Call the Coast Guard (212-668-7255) by March or so to find out the exact date. Or try Big Onion Tours (212-439-1090), an outfit that runs guided tours here on a monthly basis.

Although New York has traditionally been the country's largest and most important center of shipping, with few exceptions the great Hudson River piers that once echoed with the bustle of departing ocean liners have fallen into decline. However, you can relive an even lustier seafaring era at South Street Seaport, the twelve-block museum-without-walls that lies in the shadow of the Brooklyn Bridge. Streets are paved with Belgian blocks and lined by venerable lampposts, in a celebration of the days when tall-masted schooners docked along the East River and the air was dense with the sounds and smells of a nineteenth-century port. Masts still hover over the water, thanks to the museum's fleet of vintage sailing ships, but now the air is filled with the mating calls of beer-imbibing office workers, who flock to the area's popular bars and restaurants.

Information about current tours and special programs is available from the Visitors' Center (12 Fulton Street, telephone 212-669-9424 or 669-9400), located in the well-preserved

The Peking *at South Street Seaport*

Georgian and Federal-style commercial buildings of Scher-
merhorn Row. Plans are in the works to transform this into a
"museum with walls," where the seaport's collection of maritime artifacts would be permanently on display. For now, the
Museum Gallery on nearby Water Street features changing
exhibits on the city's seafaring past, as does the A. A. Low
Gallery, a former China merchant's counting house on John
Street.

You can watch master model makers in action at the Maritime Crafts Center and dine on seafood specialties at Sloppy Louie's and Sweet's (which, though unfortunately spruced up, date back, respectively, to the 1930s and 1800s). Browse in the stores along Cannon's Walk and in the New Fulton Market building (three floors of stores and restaurants), both on Front Street, or at Pier 17 (ditto), which stretches over the East River from behind the Fulton Fish Market. By then you'll be ready to drop on one of the old-fashioned wooden deck chairs conveniently set out on Pier 17's fourth-floor promenade. Convenient for watching river traffic pass by, they also afford an outstanding view of the *Peking*, the large and picturesque four-masted bark that's been moored next door at Pier 16 since 1975. Any remaining energy might be spent in climbing aboard for a rousing fifteen-minute film of the *Peking*'s 1929 journey around Cape Horn.

If you're in the mood for the real thing, you can actually book passage on the graceful *Pioneer,* a former cargo schooner moored nearby. The two-hour harbor cruise operates from May through September; call 212-669-9417. Or take one of the new Semi-Circle Line's ninety-minute guided daytime cruises (four daily departures) or two-hour "harbor lights" cruises that depart twice at week at 7:00 P.M. Available March through December, tickets can be purchased at the Pier 16 ticket booth and the museum visitors center. For reservations call 212-563-3200.

Ferries ran back and forth across the East River as early as 1642, but by 1800 or so, local entrepreneurs suggested that a bridge be built to connect Brooklyn with Manhattan. Eighty-three years later, the Brooklyn Bridge opened and was duly acclaimed as a masterpiece as well as the world's largest suspension bridge. Of the city's 2,000 bridges, this is by far the most famous, as well as the only one whose frequent "sale" has become a universal symbol of gullibility. Gracefully spanning the river from Park Place to Brooklyn Heights, it was designed by John Augustus Roebling, a versatile engineer who emigrated from Germany in 1831 and died in 1869 (Roebling's son, Washington, completed his father's work). The bridge also includes a pedestrian walkway that has one of the planet's most riveting views. The entrance is accessible from either Park Row or Frankfort Street, across from City Hall; the exit is at Cadman Plaza.

On the Brooklyn side, the historic Fulton Ferry District lies beneath the bridge, as does the Anchorage, a vaultlike space where summer art exhibits sometimes take place. Follow Cadman Plaza West toward the river until it turns into Old Fulton Street. Around 1816, this was known as Old Ferry Road; two years earlier, Robert Fulton's steam-powered ferries began operating between here and the other Fulton Street, on the Manhattan side of the river. The River Cafe—worth splurging on for its excellent food, celebrity-sighting opportunities, and, again, the view—sits next to the old ferry pier.

For a little afternoon music with your view, stop in at Bargemusic (718-624-4061), a former coffee barge that's been transformed into a slightly rolling venue for twice-weekly chamber music concerts. The riverfront walkway that runs up to the Manhattan Bridge from here is part of the Empire–Fulton Ferry State Park, a nine-acre urban cultural park that encompasses a block of abandoned warehouses and features an annual summer outdoor sculpture show.

A short stroll in the other direction brings you to the elegant brownstones of Brooklyn Heights, Walt Whitman's favorite neighborhood. Whitman grew up and later worked as a journalist for the *Brooklyn Eagle* here, before writing *Leaves of Grass*. Poet W. H. Auden was the unofficial landlord of an artistic boardinghouse at 7 Middagh Street, while number 24 is this historic district's oldest wooden house, dating to 1824, when the area was rolling farmland. The Brooklyn Historical

Society, based in an ornate, terra-cotta–detailed building at 128 Pierrepont Street, offers walking tours as well as an exhibit that answers the question, "What makes Brooklyn Brooklyn?" There's also a truly wonderful second-floor library. The exhibit, on the first floor, includes Casey Stengel's Brooklyn Dodger uniform, a ventriloquist's dummy from Coney Island's amusement park, and the kitchen from "The Honeymooners." For information, call 718-624-0890.

What makes Brooklyn Heights the neighborhood I'd like to call home is the riverside Promenade between Orange and Remsen streets. Built smack on top of the BQE (Brooklyn-Queens Expressway), from here Manhattan's towers take on magical proportions. When the sun goes down, the light show may remind you why you live in—or are visiting—New York in the first place.

In its own way, the aerial view from the Roosevelt Island Tramway is just as impressive. Every fifteen minutes (more often during rush hour) a red, Swiss-made tramcar leaves 59th Street and Second Avenue and rises 250 feet above the East River, silently gliding by—and over—such landmarks as the 59th Street Bridge and the Abigail Adams Smith Museum.

Four minutes later, you've arrived on what the Canarsie Indians called Minnahannock. Retagged Hog Island by early Dutch settlers, in the seventeenth century it was purchased by John Manning, an English captain later court-martialed and exiled to his home here. Not long after, ownership was transferred to a farmer named Robert Blackwell, whose family harvested fruit trees, ran a cider mill, and mined the two-mile-long island's extensive granite quarries. Between 1828 (when the city bought it) and the early 1950s, Blackwells Island, renamed Welfare Island in 1921, was home to an intriguingly awful collection of hospitals, alms houses, insane asylums, and prisons.

All this history is somewhat obscured by Roosevelt Island's current incarnation as a mainly middle-income housing development, a towering assortment of 1970s-style red brick buildings that look out at some of the East Side's poshest neighborhoods on one side and the industrial center of Queens on the other. But the gothic ruins of the smallpox hospital still stand at the island's tip. (Though officially off limits, a friend of mine says it's a great place to hunt for morel mushrooms.) Recently, it was even the inspiration for a site-specific environmental sculpture: A Japanese artist covered it with a deceptively haphazard pile of lumber, which made the century-old stone structure resemble a giant child's game of pick-up sticks. Scenic walkways edge the island's perimeters and not far from the tram dock, there's an observation pier as well as a series of "meditation steps" leading down to the river. The landmark Blackwell House, at the start of Main Street, dates to 1796 and is one of the city's oldest surviving farmhouses. Although restored in 1973, it's now used for commercial offices instead of the museum you might have hoped for. Pick up a sandwich or something and keep walking to the picnic area at Lighthouse Park, which looks north to Ward's and Randall's islands and is named, not surprisingly, for an imposing nineteenth-century lighthouse. (While officially designed by James Renwick, the architect of St. Patrick's Cathedral, local legend gives actual construction credit to one of the island's mental patients. Check out the inscription on the base and decide for yourself.)

Over the Roosevelt Island Bridge, the Socrates Sculpture Park (718-956-1819) in Long Island City is filled with large, abstract sculptures as well as seasonal flower plantings. Created in the mid-1980s from a former dump, it's definitely an example of urban renewal at its most hopeful. Not far away, the Isamu Noguchi Garden Museum (718-204-7088), housed in a converted warehouse, offers a look at this versatile artist's sculptures and collages. A high point is the small, deceptively simple garden area, where benches, stones, and various plants and trees blend together into one peaceful whole.

Close to the city's major airports and accessible by car or subway, Broad Channel is the largest of the islands that dot Queens' Jamaica Bay; a stepping stone between Howard Beach and the Rockaways that came as a revelation to me, although not, I'm sure, to local residents. A small, mainly Irish enclave where casual stilt houses jut with haphazard charm into the water, it's like stumbling across a low-rent version of Shangri-La with million-dollar views of Manhattan.

Known as "Big Egg Marsh" in the late 1800s, Broad Channel later earned the nickname "Little Cuba," possibly due to a propensity toward rum-running by local residents. Life is calmer these days, although I noticed that beer was only 30 cents a glass during "happy hour" at a pub on Cross Bay Boulevard, the community's relatively quiet main drag. "This used to be the sticks," confides a girl at Coogan's Luncheonette, where sandwiches are priced from $1.50 to $2.50 and the corner newsstand is stocked with the *Irish Voice*, the *Irish Echo*, and this week's *Racing Form*. It still seems pretty quiet; the air smells salty, people are fishing off a nearby bridge, and the biggest lure for out-of-towners is the Jamaica Bay Wildlife Refuge (see Chapter 4, "Walks on the Wild Side").

Miles away in the Bronx, City Island comes as an even bigger surprise. Maybe because this one-and-a-half-mile-long enclave was originally part of Westchester County and intended to outrival New York City as the area's fastest booming metropolis. That was back in 1760 or so, when ferries connected the island with Rodman's Neck—now part of Pelham Bay Park. By 1873, a toll bridge joined City Island with the mainland, and in 1901 a new steel bridge opened.

Ninety-some years later, the same bridge crosses over to the perfect Sunday escape: a picturesque, touristy village with a seafaring history that goes back to 1685. Along City Island Avenue, Captain Mike's Dive Training is next to City Island Bait & Tackle ("Yes! We carry foul weather gear!"); charter boats offer fishing expeditions every day at 7:00 A.M.; and dozens of restaurants advertise cut-rate seafood dinner specials.

In its heyday, City Island was famed as a major yacht-building center, several America's Cup race winners among them; the town's marinas and boatyards still sell equipment to yachts passing through on their way down to Florida or up to Rhode Island. Meanwhile, there are plenty of pretty Victorian houses and other attractions to gawk at. Drop into the City Island Historical Nautical Museum at 190 Fordham Street, open Sunday afternoons in a former schoolhouse, and you'll discover an eclectic array of treasures from precolonial times to the present.

At the North Wind Museum, back on City Island Avenue, the focus is on environmental education and "interspecies cooperation," and the atmosphere—enhanced by the ship's figurehead perched on the red roof and the old diving bells by the entrance—is definitely Jules Verne–ish. Inside, a towering set of nine-foot gray whale jaws stands next to rows of cases filled with scrimshaw, sperm-whale teeth, rare seashells, and a silver tea set discovered on a diving expedition. More stuff's on display inside a nineteenth-century ship's brig, not far from a pair of ancient-looking navy diving suits. To see it all, book the two-hour guided tour (call 718-885-0701).

A left out the museum door takes you to Hawkins Park, where three black seal statues frolic by a World War II monument; next door, the Black Whale is a quirky, cluttered little coffee house where the back garden's odd bits of statuary make a nice setting for a cup of cappuccino. Farther along, City Island Avenue ends at a cul-de-sac that looks out at Long

Cruise around Manhattan Island on the Circle Line

Island Sound and, in the distance, the Throgs Neck Bridge. Sea gulls dip, swirl, and snatch the potato chips offered by sight-seers, while small motorboats and graceful sailing yachts pass by the small "stepping stone" islands visible to the north: Hart's Island; New York's "Potter's Field," where the poor, the destitute, and unknown are buried; High Island; Rat Island; and the Chimney Sweeps. According to Native American legend, an evil spirit, besieged by hostile forces, ran across these "stepping stones" to safety on Long Island. (Where, the legend continues, he took his vengeance by tossing rocks and boulders onto the shores of Connecticut.)

Even then, canoes were a more practical means of getting around. Later years brought European settlers, with their sloops and flat-bottomed bateaux designed for easy negotiation of the area's creeks and rivers. Today, you can take the Circle Line; call 212-563-3200 for rates and schedules. Between early March and the end of December, the red, white, and green vessels depart from Pier 83 at 42nd Street and the Hudson River on three-hour, thirty-five-mile-long narrated sight-seeing expeditions around Manhattan Island. Steaming clockwise past the twin towers of the World Trade Center, the gold-domed cupolas of the World Financial Center, the Statue of Liberty and Ellis Island, the tall ships of South Street Seaport, under the Brooklyn Bridge, and past the United Nations, the journey offers a breezy microcosm of city sight-seeing.

If you're sipping coffee in the below-deck snack bar, you might miss Gracie Mansion, where city mayors have lived since 1942. Stand on deck as Roosevelt, Ward's, then Randalls Island (where British and American snipers took potshots at each other during the Revolutionary War, and everything from jazz to cricket takes place at Downing Stadium) slip by. The boat veers into the Harlem River, then north to Spuyten Duyvil—emerging at the Hudson by Inwood Hill Park and the sunset-tinted Palisades cliffs that climb the New Jersey side of the river. Here, in 1609, Henry Hudson and his sixteen-man crew moored the sixty-three-foot *Half Moon*. Almost four centuries later, the 306-mile-long river named for the early explorer still flows undaunted from the Adirondacks down to New York Bay.

Sailing Away

Each September, graceful sloops, schooners, ketches, and yawls sail from the Fireboat Pier at the tip of Battery Park out to the Verrazano-Narrows Bridge and back, filling New York Harbor with billowing sails. You could almost be in another century. Now held under the auspices of the South Street Seaport Museum, the Mayor's Cup Regatta has been an annual event for over twenty-seven years—and spectators generally book early for a place onboard the sightseeing boat which departs from Pier 16 at the seaport in time to follow the fleet. Call 212-669-9417 for this year's date and other information.

If learning how to sail is your goal, from April to October the Offshore Sailing School on City Island offers beginner and advanced classes, plus courses on racing, bareboat, and coastal cruising—even a jitney service between Manhattan and City Island (weekend classes only). Call 1-800-221-4326.

In Brooklyn, the Sheepshead Bay Sailing School offers two-hour group lessons for beginner, intermediate, and advanced sailors. Private lessons are also available. All boats leave from the Miramar Yacht Club on Emmons Avenue. For information, call 718-377-5140. Sheepshead Bay's "main drag," and the heart of Brooklyn's fishing community, Emmons Avenue is also where you'll find a fleet of noncommercial fishing boats, like the *Zephyr V*, which embarks from Pier I every morning (and also offers moonlight cruises in the harbor). Call Captain Butch at 718-743-6170; drop into Mike's Bait and Tackle (718-646-9261) to check on fishing conditions;

or just come down before dawn and walk by the docks, where dozens of charter boats are lined up, in a piscatory version of Central Park's horse-drawn carriages.

Thanks to the city's Department of Parks and Recreation, New York is the first metropolis in the country to provide adventurous kayakers and canoeists with launch sites at several strategic locales. If paddling by the bows of freighters or shooting the rapids of the East River's Hell Gate is your idea of fun, write the Metropolitan Canoe & Kayak Club (P.O. Box 021868, Brooklyn, NY 11202-0040). For permits call the Parks Department at 212-360-8133.

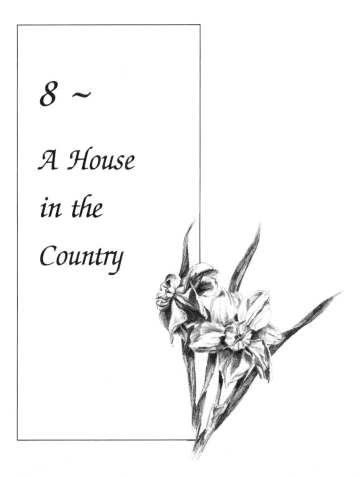

8 ~

A House in the Country

When you're longing to get out of town, don't have a weekend place of your own, or lack the time or money to go far, it's good to know that the city is filled with cottages, houses, and mansions that are open to the public—and make great getaways any time of year.

Some of the most secluded are in the north Bronx, with parklike settings ideal for picnics or a stroll in a nearby garden. Van Cortlandt House, at Broadway and 242d Street in Van Cortlandt Park, is a good example. Built in 1748 by Frederick Van Cortlandt, son of a leading New Amsterdam merchant, it was the center of a sprawling wheat plantation that included herds of cattle and sheep, as well as pigs, ducks, geese, turkeys, and other poultry.

Fields where wheat and corn rippled in the wind are now a popular spot for summer cricket matches, but the staid fieldstone manor still stands in a cluster of shady maple and linden trees, not far from the park's visitors' center. An eighteenth-century-style herb garden blooms amidst brick walkways outside the house; inside, the period rooms look so authentic you might imagine the owners have stepped out for a walk. In fact, various Van Cortlandt descendants lived here until 1889, when they sold the property to the city. A museum since 1896, many of the family's original possessions are still in place, including formal portraits, a mahogany bureau in one of the parlors, and the Chinese porcelain dinner plates and silver-encased wine bottles in the dining room where, in keeping with their status as well-connected members of early New York society, the Van Cortlandts hosted many prominent people of the time.

George Washington, though not invited, strode the wide-planked floors on more than one Revolutionary occasion: In 1776, just before the Battle of White Plains, he used the house for his military headquarters. In 1783, he stopped by again, on his way back to reclaim New York from the British, and probably slept in one of the well-furnished second-floor bedchambers. Tours are offered most weekdays and weekends by members of the Van Cortlandt volunteer corps (call 718-543-3344); the house can be easily reached by the IRT #1 train to 242d Street.

West of Van Cortlandt Park, Riverdale, with its narrow, tree-lined streets, ivy-covered brick apartment towers, and castlelike mansions, comes as a welcome surprise. JFK attended the Riverdale Country School from fourth to sixth grades (before his family moved on to the even more exclusive town of Bronxville, over the Westchester border) and "country churches," like the one on the corner of West 252d Street, add to this upscale enclave's remarkably nonurban atmosphere. Then there's Wave Hill, a nineteenth-century Greek Revival mansion surrounded by twenty-eight acres of lawns, woodlands, and stunningly beautiful gardens.

Only twenty minutes by car from midtown, and the centerpiece of the city-owned Wave Hill Environmental Center, the great stone house dates to 1844 and, over the years, has been called home by such historical figures as Teddy Roosevelt and Arturo Toscanini. Mark Twain lived here between 1901 and 1904, wistfully observing that the peacefully bucolic atmosphere made him ". . . want to live here always." Even today the rolling lawns and magnificent view of the Hudson and New Jersey's tree-edged Palisades may make you want to linger as long as possible.

Art exhibits with natural themes are presented in the main-house galleries and the turn-of-the-century Glyndor Mansion, a short walk away. Jazz and chamber music concerts are held in the Armor Hall, a medieval-ish wing built by a former curator of armor at the Metropolitan Museum. And in summer, the estate is the setting for a series of dreamy, site-specific dance performances that incorporate the trees, rills, and outdoor sculpture dotted around the grounds. All of which adds up to enough culture to satisfy the most jaded city-dweller, plus the extra delight of a ramble through ten acres of woods (which abut the northern part of Riverdale Park), a stroll in the rock-crested wild garden, where masses of artfully cultivated shrubs and wildflowers grow in shaggy abundance, and a tour of the greenhouse and gardens. Call 718-549-3200 for directions by subway and bus or details about special events and exhibitions.

At the northeast tip of Pelham Bay Park, where Long Island Sound borders a rock-strewn coast, the Bartow-Pell Mansion is the last survivor of a series of upscale residences that made this area a chillier (and much older) version of Palm Beach. At the end of a long driveway so hidden that the woman directing traffic at the Split Rock Golf Course—just a few hundred feet up Shore Road—wasn't sure where it was, the mansion was built between 1836 and 1842 as a "country seat" for Robert Bartow, a descendant of Thomas Pell (see Chapter 2, "Major Parking").

A few steps from the front gate is the "treaty tree," beneath which Pell purchased his vast tract of land from the Siwanoy Indians. Farther on, you will see a well-preserved carriage house, which opened recently as an education center and features exhibits on various old-fashioned modes of transport. But it's the handsome, Greek Revival-style stone house that really gives you the feeling that you've stepped back in time.

The interior decor, a blend of Greek Revival and American Empire with a dash of French and English classicism, is very grand and very formal, yet totally liveable. Dining room walls are painted in the deep, vibrant colors popular in the mid-nineteenth century. A freestanding staircase floats up to the third floor from the well-appointed foyer; the master bedroom's regal mahogany bed, draped in thick folds of cascading red satin, was fashioned by Charles Lannuier, a French furniture designer who opened a shop in New York back in 1803. A Savonnerie rug covers the floor of the adjoining bedroom, while down the hall, the floor of a child's room is scattered with fragile antique toys.

Appropriately, proper afternoon teas are sometimes served in the L'Orangerie, an airy, plant-filled indoor porch built over the original greenhouse by the International Garden Club. "They aren't really a garden club," a helpful docent tells me, explaining that, almost eighty years ago, this group of well-to-do socialites was instrumental in rescuing the house from ruin. Horticulturally inclined or not, they also designed the back garden, where manicured lawns run down to the woods on both sides of a central pool and fountain lined by benches—a perfect spot to sit and fantasize that you're the lord or lady of the manor. To reach the Bartow-Pell Mansion, you can either take the Lexington Avenue IRT #6 train to Pelham Bay, then walk (it's about two miles) or, Monday through Saturday, catch the #45 Westchester Bee-line bus to the front gate. Call for more directions or information about Sunday concerts, teas, and seasonal programs, 718-885-1461.

At the opposite end of the city, Staten Island is another treasure trove of country houses. Perhaps the prettiest is the gingerbread-trimmed-and-trellised waterside cottage on Hylan Boulevard in Rosebank, a pleasant neighborhood that's a short bus ride from the ferry terminal and a mile or so north of the Verrazano-Narrows Bridge. "It's a wonderful place for a picnic," confides a local resident. "But sometimes my husband and I just go and sit in the garden, and admire the view."

Even the name—Clear Comfort—is welcoming, although the cottage is better known as the Alice Austen House in honor of the pioneering woman photographer who lived here from 1866 to 1945. Selections from her 7,000-plus photographs are regularly exhibited inside, where there's also a video presentation about her life as well as knowledgeable tour guides who take you into the ornate Victorian parlor and other carefully restored rooms.

Dress-up nineteenth-century teas and other events are held in the Victorian garden, now replanted with the same varieties of flowers and weeping mulberry trees that grew in Alice's time. Like the interior of the house, the garden's original look was captured for posterity by her camera—along with the local social scene and more serious subjects, such as the lives of turn-of-the-century immigrants. The Alice Austen House Museum is open Thursday to Sunday; for directions call 718-816-4506.

Clear Comfort, Alice Austen's House

"Vous parlez Français?" asked the friendly but obviously new-immigrant driver of the taxi I mistakenly caught at the ferry terminal, as we barrelled the wrong way round the island, past buildings that have seen better days, rusty metal fences, a couple of dingy luncheonettes, and the Son Rise Interfaith Church. Turning left before the Bayonne Bridge span to New Jersey, where weeds grow rampant next to piles of junked cars, we drove through a neighborhood of small houses draped with American flags before finally, just beyond a sign for the Staten Island Mall, reaching the turnoff for "Richmond Town Restoration."

Recently renamed, Historic Richmond Town would come as an eye-opener anywhere. Here in the nation's largest city, it's like discovering that time warps actually do exist: an entire country village—once the island's main settlement—preserved, restored, and opened to the public. [It's also handily accessible by the same S-74 bus that takes you to the Jacques Marchais Center of Tibetan Art (see Chapter 5, "Gardens of Urban Delight") and High Rock Park.]

Some of the seventeenth-, eighteenth-, and nineteenth-century structures scattered throughout the 100-acre site have been moved from elsewhere on the island. A few have stood in the same spot for over three centuries. In July and August, twice-daily tours of the Voorlezer's (Schoolteacher's) House, built by the Dutch Reform Church in 1695, are conducted by bonneted, hoop-skirted guides. One of whom explains that this was where colonial children were taught their Bible and alphabet, then adds that, with the exception of local day care and other school-age groups, "even people on Staten Island who live two blocks away have never been here."

From the General Store's displays (an ancient fox skin, bolts of faded calico, canisters of chewing tobacco, and other well-preserved antique merchandise) to the spiffy little Historical Museum inside what was, until 1920, the Richmond County Clerk's and Surrogate's Office, it's worth the trip.

Stephens General Store in Richmond Town

"They're making biscuits!" shouted an older man from the window of the Guyon-Lake-Tyson House, where open-hearth baking and other forgotten domestic arts are demonstrated. Up the hill at the Stephens-Black House—a prosperous, Greek Revival–style residence with a small flower garden out back— three or four young girls in period costumes, here for the summer-apprentice program, were diligently working on their needlepoint; next door at the Tinsmith Shop, a teenage boy was learning how to fashion the mugs and coffeepots displayed for sale in a glass-enclosed case.

If your tastes run more toward miniature butter churns or hand-dipped beeswax candles, there's a gift shop in the back of the Third County Courthouse. The dignified, white-colonnaded brick structure is also the Visitor Center, where you pay admission and find out about special events that range from Halloween campfires and Victorian masquerade balls to Christmastime candlelight tours. A small café operates in the cellar of a nearby merchant's house, but when the weather's fine you can simply stretch out a blanket on the clover-covered hill that's part of the museum's picnic area. For more details, call 718-351-1611.

The SIRT (Staten Island Rapid Transit) train's last stop is the quaint little town of Tottenville, at the island's southern-most tip, where Raritan Bay meets the Arthur Kill and the Conference House sounds like a place where high-level exec-utives get together to discuss corporate mergers. In fact, on September 11, 1776, Benjamin Franklin, John Adams, and a South Carolinian named Edward Rutledge met here with Lord Richard Howe, vice admiral of the British fleet, to talk over peaceful terms for an end to the American Revolution. The hoped-for settlement didn't result (the Americans refused the British offer of a pardon), but Lord Howe proved a gracious host. According to one account, he provided his guests with "good Claret, good Bread, cold Ham, Tongues and Mutton."

Close to a century old when the meeting took place, the low-slung, two-story stone manor was more familiarly called Billop House, after the British naval captain who, according to legend, "won" Staten Island from New Jersey (see Chapter 7, "City Islands") and built his home here between 1670 and 1680. During the War of Independence, the house was used as a barracks by British troops and over ensuing centuries served as a farmhouse, a tenement, and a glue factory before finally, after years of neglect, being restored and opened as a museum in 1937.

Faded oriental rugs are scattered on the floors, and visitors can view an old sea chest that belonged to the Billop family, an embroidered canopy over one of the beds, and other sturdy pieces of colonial-era furniture. When you've finished exploring, wander down to the water's edge, or through the pungent herb and rose gardens. Special exhibits and other events take place here, too; call 718-984-2086.

A lesser-known—at least these days—Revolutionary War figure was Rufus King, an outspoken opponent of slavery, member of the Continental Congress, signer of the Constitution, two-time ambassador to Great Britain, New York's first U.S. senator, and an unsuccessful candidate for president. Somewhat of a romantic, too: Nineteen years after spending his honeymoon in the rural village of Jamaica, the New England–born King returned to Queens and bought his wife a small farmhouse that was surrounded by ninety acres of woods and fields.

Over the years, the house was expanded and added onto until it became an impressive white-columned country mansion that incorporates various Federal, Greek Revival, and Georgian architectural details. It also stayed in the King family until 1896; two years later, ownership was transferred to the city, which has kept it open to the public as a museum since the turn of the century. At the corner of 150th Street and

Jamaica Avenue, the recently restored King Manor is now the heart of an eleven-acre park—part of the original farm—that combines community events and educational workshops with exhibits on Rufus King's life and times. The oak trees he planted still tower over the grounds, and an afternoon here is a welcome urban escape. Call 718-291-0282 (weekdays) for directions and more information.

Two of King's sons married daughters of Archibald Gracie, a well-to-do Scottish immigrant who made a fortune as a shipping merchant and—to prove it—in 1799 built a grand, Federal-style mansion in the upper Manhattan countryside. There, Mr. Gracie and his wife entertained prominent friends like the Marquis de Lafayette, Washington Irving, and a future king of France, until financial setbacks forced them to sell the estate in 1823.

After going through a couple of major renovations (at one point, it was the site of the Museum of the City of New York), the gracious, pale-yellow house at 88th Street and East End Avenue became official home to New York City's mayors in 1942. Looking out over Hell Gate's choppy spasm of dangerous currents (where the East River meets the Harlem River), Gracie Mansion has also been open to the public—by appointment only, call 212-570-4751—since the 1970s. And unless you're planning to be invited to an official function in the near future, a tour may be your best chance to gawk at the "swellegant" collection of historic New York paintings and antique furniture—including a rosewood sideboard in the dining room that belonged to the Gracies—tastefully clustered inside.

The mayor's abode may be Manhattan's best known "country house," but there are others waiting to be explored. Up in Washington Heights, an imposing white-columned, Palladian-style edifice stands proudly, if oddly out of place, at the corner of West 160th Street and Edgecombe Avenue. The

Morris-Jumel Mansion, built eleven years before the American Revolution, was originally intended as a summer home for a British colonel named Roger Morris and his well-born wife, Mary Philipse, a lady once courted by the young George Washington.

If George didn't get the girl, at least he got the house—albeit temporarily. During the Battle of Haarlem Heights, he commandeered it as the Continental Army's headquarters; after the war, it became a tavern called Calumet Hall, the first stop on the Albany Post Road, where he celebrated with several of his most prominent cronies. In 1810, the house was purchased and restored by Stephen Jumel, a wealthy French merchant whose new bride and former mistress, Eliza, led a life wild enough for contemporary tabloid headlines. Because her checkered past (rumored to have included bearing an illegitimate son to a British army officer) kept them from being accepted by local society, the Jumels moved to Paris.

There, Madame Jumel managed to embroil herself in various Napoleonic intrigues until annoyed French officials exiled her back to New York, where her beleaguered husband soon died and she married the elderly, equally notorious Aaron Burr. Although the union barely lasted five months—Eliza continued to live here alone, rich, and progressively more eccentric, until her death in 1865, at the age of ninety-one—many of the French Empire furnishings she brought back from Paris still grace the nine restored period rooms. And, say guides, her ghost is sometimes seen wafting through the hallways, perhaps checking to ensure that such prize possessions as an ornate mahogany bed that belonged to Napoleon, a pair of chairs once owned by the Queen of Holland, and the dining room's delicate array of imported china and crystal are still intact. For when to go and how to get there, call 212-923-8008.

Close to the heart of midtown, just beyond the Rolls-Royce showroom that's east of First Avenue at 61st Street, the unwary pedestrian comes across a startling sight: a rustic stone house backed by a pair of looming office buildings. "The Abigail Adams Smith Museum" reads the white wood sign posted in the pocket-size front yard. "Open Monday to Friday, 12:00 P.M. to 4:00 P.M., Sunday 1:00 P.M. to 5:00 P.M."

Like other neighborhood residents, I walked by for years without seeing it. "That's what everyone says," one of the volunteer docents who leads tours of the museum tells me. The house has stood here since 1799, first as a stable, then as a popular country hotel, a private home, and much later a turn-of-the-century storage facility for the local gas company. Rescued in 1924, it's been open to the public since 1939, a reminder of the now distant time when this part of Manhattan was a fashionable rural retreat, and Colonel William Smith, President John Adams's dashing if financially feckless son-in-law, planned an "ornamental" coach house and stable as part of a grand, twenty-three-acre riverside estate. (He ran short of funds before he could finish.)

Despite a roar of traffic from the Queensborough Bridge, the pocket-size back garden's spring burst of hyacinths manages to hint at what was once a landscape of rolling meadows and orchards. From 1826 to 1833, when this was the Mount Vernon Hotel, day-trippers arrived by boat from Fulton Street to dine on green turtle soup prepared from turtles kept in an East River pen. The roomy kitchen—originally a dirt-floored shelter for pigs and cows—still looks as if it could handle a lunch order or two. Stocked with an impressive array of eighteenth- and nineteenth-century implements, it includes a foot warmer handy for brisk winter buggy rides.

Portraits of Colonel Smith and his wife, Abigail, hang over a fireplace in one of two elegantly appointed upstairs parlors; where carriages rolled up a ramp through a (now) bricked-up entranceway, there's a room devoted to historic memorabilia, like a letter written to a young Abigail from her father. In the adjoining bedroom, amidst a collection of linen coverlets, is a fine white muslin dress she made. Most of the other authentic period furnishings in the house also reflect the Federal era, but the museum is currently undergoing a one-room-at-a-time "reinstallation" designed to turn the clock forward to its later hotel incarnation. For current hours and a schedule of events (including country dance cotillions), call 212-838-6878.

Another forgotten "country" residence is tucked next to a vacant lot on East Fourth Street. Between Lafayette Street and the Bowery, around the corner from the Public Theater on Astor Place, barely east of nebulous Noho (North of Houston)—and not far from eternally funky St. Mark's Place—the Old Merchant's House, dating back to 1832, is one of those rare survivors that brings the past to the present with an incongruous jolt.

In 1835, fed up with the city's noise and pollution, a successful hardware dealer named Seabury Tredwell moved his family to the fashionable suburbs around Washington Square. Mr. Tredwell had an easy commute to his South Street office from his new home at 29 East Fourth, via the trolley car that ran along the Bowery. Then one of the best addresses in town, by the time he died in 1865, the Bowery's mansions had been replaced by beer halls, flophouses, and gangs of roving toughs; Fourth Street had become a notorious red-light district; and most of the Tredwell's upper-middle-class neighbors had long since fled. But the family stayed on, well into the twentieth century—until 1933, in fact, when Gertrude, the spinster youngest daughter, died at the age of ninety-three. Due to the intercession of a distant cousin , the house miraculously survived: Like a fly trapped in amber, the family's furniture, their clothes, even tickets to long-ago opening-night galas are on display to the public from Sunday to Thursday (call 212-777-1089 for exact times).

As you step through the ground-floor entrance, you're transported to a world where servants, responding to a bell panel in the kitchen, delivered hot tea, or perhaps a glass of fine imported sherry, to the appropriate room. Up a red carpeted stairway, the adjoining dining room and parlor's heavy red drapes and ponderous Victorian furniture are souvenirs of Mrs. Tredwell's fit of mid-nineteenth-century redecorating, while two comfortable second-floor bedrooms are crammed with the relics of the family's comfortable, nineteenth-century middle-class life: a photograph of the Tredwells on vacation at Niagara Falls, a closet full of lacy white dresses, Gertrude's graduate certificate from Mrs. Sylvanus Reed's school, dated June 16, 1869. Windows look out at a backyard that's a mere shadow of the days when it was bordered by a picket fence, planted with apple trees, and edged the open farmland that marked the outer limits of the city. The house itself, however, is so well preserved you can almost smell the wild, sweet scent of apple blossoms—and picture Gertrude Tredwell as she lived out her life in flickering gaslight, while the rest of the world changed around her.

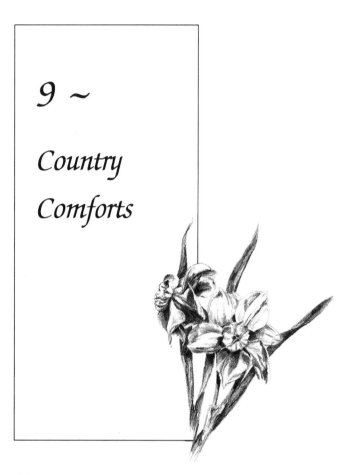

9 ~

Country Comforts

City Inns

Centuries have passed since George Washington dined at Calumet Hall, or since the Blue Bell Tavern at 181st Street and Broadway offered stagecoach travelers overnight respite from the bumps and jolts of the old Post Road. You can, however, still find a certain innlike charm at the turn-of-the-century Hotel Wales, in the Carnegie Hill section of upper Manhattan. The narrow halls, gleaming with newly restored oak paneling, lead to small, understated rooms vaguely reminiscent of old English seaside resorts: plain white walls, comfortable chairs, a substantial oak desk, the occasional (nonworking) fireplace, even tiny kitchens. Unlike those in hermetically sealed high-rise hotels, the wood-trimmed windows here actually open; in some of the cozy corner suites, they also offer treetop views of Central Park's northern reaches. A civilized afternoon tea is served amidst large potted palms in the second-floor Pied Piper Room, where chamber music concerts soothe city-rattled souls on Sunday afternoons, and mornings start with coffee, tea, and blueberry muffins. Or splurge on a real country breakfast at Sarabeth's Kitchen, on the ground floor. Rates start at $145, afternoon tea, and continental breakfast included. 1295 Madison Avenue (at 92nd Street), New York, NY 10128. Tel. 212-876-6000.

The Boxtree is best known as an exquisitely opulent restaurant in Manhattan's midtown Turtle Bay area. But since 1987 the top floors of its two elegant brownstones have also housed the Boxtree Hotel, a "city inn" with the rarified air of a country château. Though each of the lavish rooms and suites has a different theme—from English country garden to mock Egyptian—all have working fireplaces, luxurious marble bathrooms, and Australian possum throws on the beds (four-posters in the penthouse suites). And while hallway trompe l'oeil murals of garden gates, birds, and flowers may help guests forget they're in New York City, the (almost) twenty-four-hour room service and $100 dining voucher good at the formal dining room (there's also a more casual bistro) are sure to remind them. Rates start at $250, including continental breakfast. 250 East 49th Street, New York, NY 10017. 212-758-8320.

Incentra Village House may be Manhattan's closest approximation of a casual rural hostelry. You get your own key, have your own outside doorbell, and make your own breakfast when you stay in this adjoining pair of nineteenth-century houses, which overlook a quiet stretch of Eighth Avenue between 12th and Jane (two of the Village area's prettiest streets). Rooms range from suites to a converted stable and feature working fireplaces, kitchenettes, and names that match their found-in-the-attic decor. The Maine Room has a large double four-poster bed and matching bureau that came from a Maine farmhouse; the red, white, and blue Washington Room features a brass bed and sleeping loft that might suit a family. Guests—who tend to stay anywhere from four days to three months—can also relax in the stylish double-parlor, which has two fireplaces, Oriental rugs, and a baby grand piano used for Saturday evening recitals. Although a large proportion of its clientele is gay, Incentra also welcomes grandparents, children, and dogs. "We're very open and liberal-minded," says the owner. Rates start at under $100. 32 Eighth Avenue, New York, NY 10014. 212-206-0007.

Not far from the Greenmarket at Union Square, Chelsea Inn, on the top three floors of another pair of adjoining townhouses, offers a choice of suites and single rooms, all with kitchenettes, daily maid service, and free local phone calls. Some rooms share a bath; all are unabashedly flea market in decor. ("Is this what you call funky?" asked a recent guest from the suburbs.) The inn is especially popular with young overseas visitors and other independent spirits who enjoy the freedom of having a key to the front door. "People that like it, love it," the desk clerk tells me. "It's like staying at a friend's house." Rates start at under $100. 46 West 17th Street, New York, NY 10011. 212-645-8989.

Just a block from South Street Seaport, Best Western Seaport Inn is the only hotel in town that actually calls itself a country inn. The renovated nineteenth-century warehouse has sixty-five rooms decorated with Federalist-style cherry-wood antiques, as well as modern amenities like VCRs and minifridges. Rooms on the sixth floor also have Jacuzzis and terraces with views of the Seaport, the Brooklyn Bridge, even Brooklyn Heights and Governors Island. Peck Slip, it's worth noting, was named for prominent merchant Benjamin Peck, whose portrait hangs in the Museum of the City of New York's Marine Gallery. Rates start at $150. 33 Peck Slip, New York, NY 10038. 212-766-6600 or 800-HOTEL-NY.

Other hostelries with innlike flavor include the Washington Square Hotel (212-777-9515) which, as the old Hotel Earle, attracted more than its share of raffish Village residents. Spruced-up several years back, some rooms, though small, overlook the trees in Washington Square. Rates start at under $100. The more expensive Sheraton Park Avenue (212-685-7676) is in Murray Hill, and stands on land once occupied by Robert Murray's farm. As the Russell Hotel, it counted Calvin Coolidge's widow among its residential guests. Though not exactly "country," its 150 rooms and suites offer a certain quiet, English-club-style spaciousness.

Bed and breakfasts are an increasingly popular hotel alternative even in Manhattan, with two of the most reliable local services being the Bed & Breakfast Network of New York (212-645-8134) and City Lights Bed and Breakfast (212-737-7049). Both offer rooms in apartments and houses for prices that range up from $50 per night. The Fund for the Borough of Brooklyn has listings of several bed and breakfasts including Foy House, an 1894 Park Slope brownstone that's only ten minutes away from attractions like the Brooklyn Museum and Botanic Gardens. Call the Fund at 718-855-7882.

Country Restaurants

When it comes to dining out(side), New Yorkers have a choice of venues: The Boathouse Cafe, Tavern on the Green's sylvan terrace, or anywhere else in Central Park (especially the Great Lawn, during summer concerts). They can also dine alfresco at the top floor promenade of Pier 17 at South Street Seaport (the floor below is a mecca of intriguing food outlets) or the café at Wave Hill, the Bronx, where a breezy terrace overlooks the Hudson.

On the low-key side, there's Greenacre Park, at East 51st Street between Second and Third avenues. Reservations are definitely not required—as the sign by the entrance puts it, this is "a private park for public enjoyment." Almost all year round, you can sit at tables under a sheltered side patio (heating elements in the roof keep the air toasty even in December) and enjoy an inexpensive breakfast or lunch—even dinner, if your taste runs to soup, sandwiches, or a giant rice-and-bean burrito—to the roar of a cascading waterfall.

Sarabeth's Kitchen started with a jar of homemade orange-apricot marmalade and grew into three Manhattan restaurants: on the Upper West Side (423 Amsterdam Avenue at 80th Street, 212-496-6280); inside the Whitney Museum (945 Madison, 212-570-3670); and on the ground floor of the Hotel Wales (1295 Madison at 92nd St., 212-410-7335), an airy, green-carpeted establishment where the decor—paintings of cows and barns—goes well with the breakfast/brunch menu's farmer's omelette, pumpkin waffles, and, of course, bevy of delicious homemade jams and bread.

After a morning at the Union Square Greenmarket, try lunch at Friend of a Farmer, 77 Irving Place (212-477-2188). Oil lamps hang from the ceiling, jars of beans line shelves, floors are scattered with baskets of pumpkins and winter squash, and the casual fare includes full country breakfasts, a ranch-hand special meatloaf for lunch, and the farmer's cold platter for dinner. They also sell home-baked breads, pies, and cookies, to go.

Union Square Greenmarket

The Union Square Cafe (21 East 16th Street, 212-243-4020) is only a few blocks away but it might be light-years in terms of sophisticated ambience. A posh, three-tiered restaurant frequented by some of the city's sleekest writers, publishers, and agents, the cuisine here is pricey, innovative Italian-French, and, as much as possible, prepared using produce from the Greenmarket. They also offer a popular Greenmarket lunch. Reservations are suggested here and at the Hudson River Club (250 Vesey Street, 212-786-1500), which is located in the World Financial Center and specializes in venison, rabbit, and other delicacies from the state's Hudson Valley region.

On the corner of St. Luke's Place—a gently curving row of nineteenth-century townhouses—Anglers and Writers (420 Hudson Street, 212-675-0810) is the kind of café where you feel entirely comfortable whiling away an afternoon with a book and a steaming cup of cappuccino. Or, if you've forgotten to bring something to read, pick up the complete works of Tennessee Williams and Bernard Shaw from a nearby bookshelf. Antiquated fishing gear hangs on the walls, bunches of wildflowers are set on mismatched tables, and the leather-bound menu lists such reasonably priced and homely items as hearty harvest soup, old-fashioned stew, and bourbon-glazed country ham.

A short walk away, the Grange Hall (50 Commerce Street, 212-924-5246), is in the heart of Greenwich Village, where streets have narrowed down to lanes lined by shady trees. Edna St. Vincent Millay once lived in a narrow sliver of a house on nearby Bedford Street, and photographer Berenice Abbott lived upstairs when this was the Blue Mill Tavern, a speakeasy-turned-restaurant run by the same family for two generations. Now the emphasis is on American farm food: Mohegan succotash, Amish potato salad, steak with yam fries, while the drink selection ranges from root beer and orange soda pop to "prairie martinis" and hot buttered rum.

You don't need to go to Texas for country western chow, although Cowgirl Hall of Fame (519 Hudson Street, 212-633-1133) happens to be officially connected with the National Cowgirl Hall of Fame in Texas. Tables are dressed in red-checked cloths; antler chandeliers hang from the ceiling here and in the adjoining bar, which is lined by faux cowhide-covered stools. The cowgirl of the moment (it changes every two months) is honored in the wood-paneled lounge, a few steps from a private dining room adorned with photos of champion women bronc riders. Start off with a few fried cat-fish fingers, dip into some branding-iron barbecued chicken, tuck into an order of bunkhouse steak, then wash it all down with a Sioux City sarsaparilla.

There's an idealized view of a mountain lake painted on one wall of Saranac (1350 Madison Avenue, 212-289-9600), an uptown restaurant whose upstate Adirondacks Lodge decor is enhanced by a deer-antler chandelier that hangs from the ceiling, along with an upside-down toboggan and canoe. Wooden booths are lit by yellow parchment lamps that give the cream-colored walls a glow as cozy as the country-casual menu's meatloaf, chicken pot pie, and homemade apple pie almost as good as Mom used to make.

Another East Side eatery where the food and atmosphere is distinctly nonurban is Lion's Rock (316 East 77th Street, 212-988-3610), where each of two intimate brick-walled dining rooms has its own wood-burning fireplace. What really gives diners a breath of fresh air, however, is the back garden's wood fence, flower bed, and towering red granite rock—a favorite picnic spot for courting couples in the nineteenth century, when this was part of Jones Woods, a wild, craggy region that stretched from here down to 68th Street. Today, the restaurant's picnic basics include grilled veal chops, roasted chicken breast, and a Sunday brunch of waffles and smoked brook trout.

At Fraunces Tavern restaurant (212-269-0144), on the corner of Pearl and Broad streets, you can feast on a prix-fixe "colonial repast" that includes clam chowder made from a 1789 recipe. For an even more historic eating experience, be adventurous and book one of the eighteenth-century Tavern Nights that are held occasionally at the Queens County Farm Museum. Using documented recipes, food is cooked on an open hearth and served by staff in authentic period clothing; even the tableware is historically accurate. On Staten Island, Historic Richmond Town presents a series of carefully researched, traditional nineteenth-century dinners that start with a round of cool cider and end with a game of skittles or dice, accompanied by music of the 1830s played by musicians in appropriate period costumes; and, on Saturday nights between January and April, the village tavern becomes a candlelit setting for evenings of traditional folk music.

Country Music

A few years back, Randy Travis bought a Guild dreadnought guitar from Mandolin Brothers, a Staten Island company that's one of the world's largest dealers of vintage and new American fretted instruments. More recently, Radio City Music Hall Productions hosted "Country Takes Manhattan," a ten-day series of concerts by Dolly Parton, Willie Nelson, Clint Black, and Wynonna Judd—at venues ranging from Carnegie Hall to Central Park's Summerstage—that may become an annual event. And it might come as a surprise to learn that WYNY-FM (103.5 on your dial) is not only the city's only country music station, but at over a million listeners a week, it's also got the largest audience of any country station, anywhere.

For live music, try the Lone Star Roadhouse (212-245-2950) on West 52nd Street, where New York bands like the World Famous Blue Jays rock with a country beat, and if you're lucky, you might hear Jerry Jeff Walker. Bands play every night at the Rodeo Bar (212-683-6500), a Third Avenue hangout where the bar's a converted horse trailer. Country western music is occasionally featured at Tramps (212-727-7788), a loftlike Chelsea space that stays open until at least 4:00 A.M.; and sometimes a bluegrass band or two holds forth at the Eagle Tavern (212-924-0275), a traditional Irish music bar on West 14th Street that's as casual as dropping into someone's living room.

There's a country dance party every August during the Lincoln Center Out-of-Doors festival (212-875-5400), and square dancing on Thursday nights at the Queens County Farm Museum, as well as during the City Gardeners' Harvest Festival—where the country music highlight is the New York City Bluegrass Band & Banjo Contest (718-427-3221). An event that over a period of twenty-plus years has taken place— always in mid-August—at various locales around the city (from South Street Seaport to Snug Harbor), the contest has been an integral part of the harvest festival for the last eight or so. Even a torrential downpour one year couldn't keep at least 600 avid fans from packing the contest's yellow-striped tent to hear bluegrass bands from as far away as Russia, and as close as Brooklyn.

10 ~

Fairs and
Festivals

Brooklyn's Floyd Bennett Field became New York's first municipal airport when it opened in 1931. A decade later, it was a naval air station, and during World War II, it was one of the country's busiest air terminals. Now the site of the Gateway National Recreation Area's headquarters, it's also where, every August for almost twenty years, the annual City Gardeners' Harvest Fair has attracted hordes of city folk eager for a taste of homegrown produce and down-home entertainment that ranges from genuine Brooklyn cowboys doing rope tricks to square-dance lessons. (For the exact date, call 718-338-3799.)

Sweet corn at the City Gardeners' Harvest Fair

It started small, when local gardeners harvested a crop of vegetables in a corner of the old airfield and threw a party to celebrate. But it's grown to include a bumper crop of exhibitors, from the Sierra Club to (my personal favorite) the New York Turtle and Tortoise Society. They come here from outside the city, too: During a recent fair, the Orange County Dairy Princess and Dairy Maid—two bored, blond teenagers—gave milking demonstrations, with the help of a couple of Brown Swiss cows tethered behind them. Nearby, a few reluctant ewes were being sheared, as part of a "Sheep to Shawl" exhibit. But like any good county fair, the main attraction was the bumper crop of flowers, fruits, and vegetables vying for blue ribbons in categories like "the largest tomato" and "the largest sunflower." Even the day after ribbons were awarded (when the entries were displayed in slightly wilted splendor), the tables full of city-grown harvest inspired amazed kudos from onlookers. "I never knew you could grow stuff like this in New York," murmured one woman.

Late summer and early fall is one of the peak seasons for "fair-hopping," but special events with country flavor take place throughout the year, in all five boroughs.

In September there's an annual Native American Festival at Inwood Hill Park, near the site of an Indian village that was called Shorakapok, or "edge of the river." In 1992, the festival included a formal renaming of the park's ancient forest as the Shorakapok Natural Area; every year, it includes Native American cultural events, crafts, storytelling, music, and dance. (Call the Urban Park Rangers at 212-427-4040 for the exact day.)

Also in September, the Queens County Fair (718-247-FARM) takes place on the city's only official working farm—and like the Native American Festival, has been a country milestone for more than a decade. There's everything from bluegrass music to hayrides to corn-husking and pie-eating contests, along with traditional baking, canning, and livestock competitions. In mid-October another tradition is the annual Garden Harvest Festival and Craft Fair (718-817-8700), a weekend-long event at the New York Botanical Garden that includes basket weaving, hayrides, square dancing, apple-cider pressing as well as displays of natural and botanical crafts.

When winter covers the city with a blanket of snow, it's time to head for Historic Richmond Town (718-352-1611), where December starts off with a Women's Auxiliary sale of handcrafted and home-baked goods; continues with two-hour Candlelight Tours through Richmond Town's historic seventeenth- and eighteenth-century buildings; then wraps up with the sights and smells of a nineteenth-century Christmas during the three-day Victorian Holiday Revels. Meanwhile, the Abigail Adams Smith Museum in Manhattan (212-838-6878) hosts an annual holiday-decorating workshop guaranteed to get you into another century's spirit of things. Up in the Bronx, colonial carolers and a traditional bonfire are part of the guided Candlelight Tours at the Van Cortlandt House Museum (718-543-3344).

The annual shad run up the Hudson is celebrated with a Shad Festival at Inwood Hill Park, where—every April—volunteers from the Hudson River Foundation demonstrate the proper way to cook this native fish, and visitors happily volunteer to eat them. Demonstrations of river ecology, fly fishing, ranger-led nature walks, and children's entertainment are also featured. Call 212-427-4040.

Spring is also the time of the New York Botanical Garden's annual Maple Sugar Sunday (718-817-8700) and garden open house.

Additional floral delights can be enjoyed at the Greater New York Orchid Show, which transforms the World Financial Center's Winter Garden into a bower of more than 150,000 orchids. Rockefeller Center's newly annual Flower and Garden Show includes whimsical topiaries and woodland glades. Macy's Flower Show is one of those harbingers of the season that makes you glad to be here. (Dates are listed in local newspapers.) So is the New York Flower Show, the grande dame of the city's floral displays, organized by the Horticultural

Society of New York—that turns Pier 92 (52nd Street and the Hudson River) into a kind of enchanted forest. A little later on, the same facility is where you'll find the Great American Quilt Festival, a bi-annual, five-day celebration of the quilt as art form, that's a combination of exhibit and marketplace—and co-sponsored by the Museum of American Folk Art (212-977-7170).

In July, Federal troops and Confederate rebels occupy Historic Richmond Town during the annual Civil War Encampment that culminates with a Regimental Ball (costumes are optional). On July 4, the village also hosts an old-fashioned ice-cream social during its Independence Day Celebration. At the end of July, the Thunderbird Native American Dancers' Mid-Summer Pow Wow takes place at the Queens County Farm Museum, three centuries or so after the Matinecock Indians "traded away" this part of Queens. A fund-raiser for a city-based Native American scholarship fund, each year thousands of visitors flock to watch "fancy dance" competitions, taste authentic honey-dipped Indian fry bread, and browse amidst crafts from the twenty-five or so tribes represented during the two-day event.

At the end of August, the Richmond County Fair on Staten Island is not only one of the city's biggest, but also one of its most entertaining get-togethers. Along with traditional contests for the longest zucchini and biggest tomato, there's a pig race, a bed race, frog jumping, even a "diaper derby" baby race. (For dates and details, call the Staten Island Historical Society at 718-351-1611.)

11 ~

Rainy Days, Rodeos, and Other Resources

Like anyplace else, New York has its share of rainy, miserable days. But when the city's sunk in a mist of low-hanging clouds, a visit to a museum or two can be almost as good as a walk in the woods. Strangely (or not so strangely), one of the best places to explore the great outdoors is inside the American Museum of Natural History. Built in 1874, when Central Park was a swampy miasma inhabited by goat farmers, it's home to more dinosaurs, whale skeletons, birds, and fossil mammals than any other museum on earth—and its miles of corridors magically transport you from one ecosystem to another in a matter of minutes.

Gulls are suspended from an arched ceiling of blue sky and white clouds in the Hall of Pacific Bird Life, to the right of the main entrance at Central Park West and 79th Street. On the third floor, New York City birds are frozen in perpetual flight, not far from a display on the life and customs of Eastern Woodlands Indians. Around the corner from the Teddy Roosevelt Memorial Hall, on the first floor, the Hall of North American Forests exhibit takes you from an apple orchard in upstate Dutchess County to maple-syrup making in the Catskills. Ramble through the New York Agriculture Exhibit, which progresses from forest primeval to modern farmer and even captures nature's seasons behind glass. For a much, much closer look, check out the Naturemax Theater's four-story screen or take a trip far, far out of town, at the Hayden Planetarium.

Finding your way around can be confusing, but the museum's numerous kiosks are stocked with helpful maps. Guards are also helpful when it comes to directions. "Take a right at invertebrates," one breezily informed me when I asked the way to the Whale's Lair, one of three restaurants and cafés cannily hidden around the complex. Soon I was sipping cranberry juice under a model of a ninety-four-foot-long blue whale. For hours and current exhibits call 212-769-5100.

Teddy Roosevelt's Rough Rider hat is on display in the Museum of Natural History, but the rest of his wardrobe is preserved at the Theodore Roosevelt Birthplace, a stately brownstone—and National Park site—at 28 East 20th Street. Wander around and you'll see a horsehair hatband from his cowboy days, the army canteen he drank from at San Juan Hill, and the shirt he was wearing when a would-be assassin shot him on October 14, 1912. The first-floor study, lined with stuffed lions and other deceased wild game, includes a lifelike portrait, his pith helmet, and his cowboy hat. For details, call 212-260-1616.

Take a horse-drawn carriage in Central Park

Off the east side of Central Park, the Museum of the City of New York includes six period rooms—one seventeenth-century Dutch, another mid-eighteenth-century English, still another a perfect re-creation of an 1830 drawing room furnished in "the fashionable and splendid" style New Yorkers of the time enjoyed. The museum's collection of prints offers some of the earliest views of New Amsterdam, including one of the stockade that gave Wall Street its name and a color etching of New York in 1763, by an English artist and captain in the Royal Regiment of Artillery, in which the city looks idyllic, rural, and vaguely tropical. Local seafaring history can be explored in the Marine Gallery, from the two-ton bronze statue of Robert Fulton that once graced the entrance to the Fulton Street ferryhouse in Brooklyn to dioramas of Henry Hudson and his crew aboard the *Half Moon* in 1609. There's also a fleet of almost-seaworthy ship models, but the most intriguing relic may be a figurehead of Andrew Jackson, carved for the U.S. frigate *Constitution* in 1834 and partially replaced soon after an unknown sailor sneaked on board and sawed off the head. The original was never recovered. The museum entrance is at 103d and Fifth Avenue; call 212-534-1672 for hours and information.

Only one cultural center in the city can claim that General Lafayette, hero of the American Revolution, laid its cornerstone. At least, he laid the cornerstone for the Brooklyn Apprentices' library, the Brooklyn Museum's 1825 progenitor, whose lofty aim was "to shield young men from evil associations, and to encourage improvement during leisure hours by reading and conversation." If you have endless leisure hours, you could try to take in all the million and half objects now housed in the museum's 1897 landmark building on Eastern Parkway, near the Botanic Garden. If you don't, head for the fifth floor, where the collection of Hudson River school paintings comes as a breath of fresh air, or at least makes you feel you've taken a minitrip out of town. On the fourth floor, two carefully restored Dutch colonial farmhouses take you on a journey back in time: Each was rescued from neglect and reconstructed here, shingle by shingle.

More of the city's vanishing past—in the form of bits and pieces of stone and terra-cotta architectural detail from demolished buildings—is artfully scattered in the sculpture garden at the rear. Call 718-638-5000.

Beneath the city's 6,400 miles of streets, other remnants of the past lie embedded in layers of landfill. New York Unearthed, at 17 State Street, gives you a free close-up view, thanks to an anthropomorphic creation named UeNYse (Unearthing New York Systems Elevator). A few steps from the basement conservation laboratory and excavation wall, a sign warns that this clever interactive moving theater should be avoided if you have a heart condition, a back problem, or are under the influence of alcohol or drugs. No wonder. The shakes, shudders, and jolts as UeNYse drops below the surface are amazingly realistic. So is the "window" (a 3-D screen) that allows you to gaze into an archaeological dig-in-progress. For hours, call 212-363-9372.

A Short Shopping Detour

Manhattan has been one of the world's greatest outdoor shopping malls since its early days as a trading post. Beaver, otter, mink, and wildcat skins were among the cargo shipped back to Holland onboard the *Arms of Amsterdam* in 1626. By 1643, according to accounts of the day, the open-air market at the corner of Pearl and Whitehall streets was a virtual bedlam of languages, customs, and goods.

The shopping ambience has become somewhat more sophisticated since then, but you can still find a growing number of stores that sell countrylike goods—or at least feature decors that create welcome rural illusions. Zoos, for instance, have shops filled with conveniently apartment-sized (stuffed) wild beasts; at the botanical gardens, you can buy plants, seeds, and floral English pottery; and museum stores are crammed with just about everything, from the worldwide crafts and collectibles at the Museum of Natural History to the complete works of Edith Wharton—and jewelry made from subway tokens—recently spotted for sale at the Museum of the City of New York.

The Museum of American Folk Art is not only home to one of the country's most comprehensive collections of folk painting, sculpture, textiles, and decorative furniture, it also has two shops, one on West 50th Street and the other next to the museum entrance at Two Lincoln Square (Columbus between 65th and 66th). The atmosphere here is folksy enough to warm even Will Rogers's heart: Walls are hung with weathervanes, dried floral wreaths, and framed quilt squares; shelves are lined with books on pottery and basket making; and any leftover space is crammed with carved wooden farm animals and hand-stitched ornaments (call 212-496-2966 for store hours).

H. Kauffman & Sons, at the corner of 29th Street and Park Avenue South, has been in business since 1875, and is still one of the best places (of any century) to find staid English riding attire, polo and western gear, as well as saddlebags, saddles, and bridles. Kiehl's, at Third and 13th Street, looks like the kind of old-fashioned pharmacy you'd find in a small Vermont village, and has been making its own line of natural moisturizers, cleansers, perfumes, and lotions since 1851. Frequent campers swear by Tents & Trails, down at 21 Park Place; athletic types by Eastern Mountain Sports, up at 20 West 61st; and sailors by the charts and compasses of New York Nautical

Instruments and Service Corps at 140 West Broadway in Tribeca, in operation since 1910.

A few blocks north of Tribeca, the cobblestoned byways of Soho aren't only lined by slick art galleries and haute hip cafés. They've recently sprouted a number of nouveau-country emporiums, including Terra Verde Trading Company (120 Wooster Street between Prince and Spring streets), where everything from the "barn beds" made of Northern Californian redwood to shawls woven from naturally colored cotton is unbleached, untreated, and undyed, including soaps, bath stuff, and sheets. The store's non-toxic cleaning products are almost pure enough to eat; even the birthday candles are made of natural beeswax. Nearby, Hometown (131 Wooster Street, off Prince) is a slice of vintage Americana, a place choked with the kind of stuff Grandma had and threw away: A 1920 Maine license plate, an appealingly rusted weather-vane, vintage school pennants, and a collection of perfectly preserved Little Golden Books that may take you back to your childhood (even your parents' childhood). If that doesn't work, let your imagination take flight at The Enchanted Forest (85 Mercer Street), a child's fairy-tale version of the country, with a miniature grotto, a tiny waterfall, an eerily illuminated crystal cave, and various stuffed and wooden creatures peering through a bower of gently arched trees. On the next block, After the Rain (149 Mercer Street) is a mysterious medieval country of a store, where a stone archway leads into a dimly lit space with flagstone floors, a stone fireplace, and wood plank tables on which hammered dulcimers, drums, kaleidoscopes, miniature Apache baskets, and other crafts are displayed.

Stop for lunch at Fanelli's, on the corner of Prince and Mercer (opened in 1872, it has the kind of friendly atmosphere where babies in strollers are as welcome as beer drinkers spouting poetry). Then walk west on West Houston. You'll pass right by Big Sky Western Furniture (114 West Houston), where chairs and tables made of recycled horse troughs are almost guaranteed to make your home look like Dale Evans did the decorating. From here, cross Sixth Avenue and wander the maze of winding Village lanes that lead to Lucy Anna (502 Hudson Street), one of a row of down-home stores along this West(ern) Village thoroughfare. The owner named it after her two grandmothers and says it's the "only homemade quilt store in New York." Farther along, Cowgirl Hall of Fame (519 Hudson) may be better known as one of the city's most colorful dining spots, but the "general store" wedged between the bar and restaurant has the cheeriest collection of tacky memorabilia this side of the Rio Grande. Cactus jelly, sheriff's badges, vintage clothing, even Indian blankets are all stuffed into a space the size of a good-size closet. Well-worn vintage blue jeans are the house specialty at Whiskey Dust (526 Hudson), just across the street. Duck under a steer skull and you're in a world of saddles, harnesses, old boots, and clothing, about 85 percent secondhand and broken in by gen-you-ine Montana cowpokes, plus cans of cowboy coffee and sticks of jerky chew—and cowboy hats that, if they could talk, would gab about rodeos and such.

Urban Cowboys

Rodeos, in fact, have been a staple at Madison Square Garden for over seventy years (call 212-465-6741 to find out when the next one's due to blow through town). But New York has its own homegrown version, too. The five-day Black World Championship Rodeo has been held in a Harlem park each May for the past decade, with participants from as far away as Texas and Oklahoma competing in bull riding, calf wrestling, barrel racing, and roping events. The rodeo's summer-riding program takes place at the New York City Riding Academy of

Randalls Island, and there are school programs throughout the year. For information, call 212-675-0085.

Useful Addresses

For a copy of *Parks at a Glance*, which features information on the city's 6 beaches, 13 golf courses, 40 indoor and outdoor swimming pools, 500 tennis courts, numerous riding stables, skating rinks, and playing fields (plus the rock-climbing wall at Manhattan's West 59th Street Recreation Center), call 212-360-1309 or write to the New York City Department of Parks and Recreation, Press Office, Room 311, The Arsenal, Central Park, 830 Fifth Avenue, New York, NY 10021. Ask them what other publications are available—or drop by and take a look. They're open Monday to Friday, 9:00 A.M. to 5:00 P.M.

For information about parks in a particular borough, call the parks department offices in the Bronx (718-430-1800); Brooklyn (718-965-8900); Manhattan (212-408-0201); Queens (718-520-5900); and Staten Island (718-390-8000).

To find out more about state parks in New York City, write to the New York State Office of Parks, Recreation and Historic Preservation, NYC Region, 915 Broadway, New York, NY 10010 or call 212-387-0271.

For brochures on Manhattan's seven national parks (Statue of Liberty, Ellis Island, Castle Clinton, Federal Hall, Grant's Tomb, Theodore Roosevelt's Birthplace, Hamilton Grange) write to the National Park Service, 26 Wall Street, New York, NY 10005 or call 212-264-4456.

Bibliography

Barlow, Elizabeth. *The Forests and Wetlands of New York City*. Little Brown and Co., 1971

———. *Frederick Law Olmsted's New York*. Praeger Publishing, 1972.

Botkin, B. A., ed. *New York City Folklore*. Random House, 1956.

Brierly, J. Ernese. *The Streets of Old New York*. Hastings House, 1953.

Cudahy, Brian J. *Over & Back, The History of Ferryboats in New York Harbor*. Fordham University Press, 1990.

Dunlop, David W. *On Broadway: A Journey Uptown Over Time*. Rizzoli International Publications, 1990.

Federal Writers Project. *New York Panorama*. Random House, 1938.

Finney, Jack. *Time and Again*. Simon & Schuster, 1970.

Goldstone, Harmon H. and Martha Dalrymple. *History Preserved*. Schocken Books, 1976.

Hansen, Harry. *North of Manhattan*. Hastings House, 1950.

Holbrook, Stewart. *The Old Post Road*. McGraw-Hill, 1962.

Houghton Mifflin. *Insight New York CityGuide*. 1991.

Jenkins, Stephen. *The Story of the Bronx*. G. P. Putnams' Sons, 1912.

Kieren, John. *A Natural History of New York City*. Houghton Mifflin, 1959.

Lockwood, Charles. *Manhattan Moves Up Town*. Houghton Mifflin, 1976.

Malcolm, Andrew H. *U.S. 1, America's Original Main Street*. St. Martin's Press, 1991.

McCullough, David W. *Brooklyn . . . And How It Got That Way*. The Dial Press, 1983.

Morris, Lloyd. *Incredible New York*. Random House, 1951.

Scheller, William G. *Country Walks Near New York*. Adirondack Mountain Club, 1980.

Tanner, Ogden. *Urban Wilds*. Time-Life Books, 1975.

Von Pressentin Wright, Carol, ed. *Blue Guide New York*. Norton, 1991.

White, E. B. *Here Is New York*. Warner Books, 1988.

White, Norval. *New York, A Physical History*. Atheneum, 1987.

Wilensky, Eliot and Norval White. *AIA Guide to New York City*. Harcourt Brace Jovanovich, 1988.

Index